To my Grandpa George,
whose creativity and thoughtfulness
inspired my love of homemade gifts.

SUSTAINABLE CELEBRATIONS
THAT WON'T COST THE EARTH

Green Christmas

Words and photography by

JEN CHILLINGSWORTH

Illustrated by Sophie Elm

quadrille

Contents

Introduction

Snow is falling heavily outside. As I sit at my desk, I watch as it encloses the landscape, turning everything into a sea of white. A clattering of jackdaws sits huddled on the branches of the bare oak tree, while a wood pigeon is perched on a television aerial, puffing up its wings. Traffic slows, and the town slips into silence. It's cold in the house, and I have an old woollen blanket over my legs and my warmest sweater on to help keep out the chill. A candle burns gently in the background, comforting me with its soothing scent of eucalyptus and myrtle. I sip freshly brewed coffee from my favourite cup, and I fight the urge to stare out of the window as I'm supposed to be working. Snow makes everything look beautiful, and the town is starting to resemble a picturesque Christmas card. It's easy to feel excited about the forthcoming festive period.

Christmas is when we wrap ourselves up in nostalgia. My fondest memories are of spending time with my grandpa. I was his first grandchild, and we shared a birthday, giving us a special connection from day one. He was an art teacher, good at drawing and painting, but he was also a talented ceramicist and woodworker. Every Christmas, my grandparents' house was decorated with the things he made, and I remember with fondness the snowman table settings fashioned from ping-pong balls, and an oil painting of Santa and his sleigh flying over a quirky cottage, with Rudolph the reindeer leading the way across a snowy sky. Rudolph's nose blinked on occasion, as my grandpa had attached a bulb within the picture's frame. It might sound a little tacky, but it was wonderful to me as a child. My grandpa also made gifts for me at Christmas. Once there was a hand-built wooden go-kart with a number plate (license plate) that read 'Jenny'. Another time, after pestering him endlessly about what he was getting me for Christmas, he professed that I would receive a bag of crisps. Not believing him, I was dismayed to discover in a wrapped box, a single bag of ready-salted crisps. Obviously, he was joking, and had in fact upcycled an old school desk, which I absolutely loved. These are the special gifts I remember from childhood.

As an adult, I lost my way a little. I was unhappy and as a way of coping, I shopped. Influenced by magazines, television and friends, I followed trends, buying new homeware and clothes that I felt would transform my life and make me happy. My home and wardrobe were bursting with stuff I didn't use or need. Christmas followed the same pattern. It was a season where I used to feel the urge to do everything and buy everything. After having my son, I wanted to give him the perfect holiday, spending money I didn't have to fulfil the fantasy. He would wake up on Christmas morning to a stocking bulging with gifts he hadn't asked for. In my head I felt I was a bad parent if I didn't fill that stocking with lots of extras, but my son's sole focus was on the toys he had asked for and those were the ones he played with. The rest of the stuff was relegated to the toybox and forgotten about. January would arrive, and with it, the credit card bill. Anxiety and stress would hit hard as I panicked about

how to pay for everything. This went on for years until eventually I worked out how many additional hours I would have to put in at a job I hated to pay for all the extra stuff we didn't need or really want. It was a bit of a wake-up call, and it also made me consider what our future was going to be if I continued with this lifestyle. It took many years learning how to slow down and simplify, but life is so much better.

We now approach the festive season differently. We have created our own traditions, and we look forward to them every year. In our house we read a lot, and every time one of us completes a book, we put a £1 coin in a jar. As we approach the holidays, we tally up all the coins and head into town to buy new books from our local bookshop. We go in the early evening, so we can walk through our neighbourhood and admire the decorations in the windows and gardens, and enjoy the town lit up for Christmas. After selecting new books to read over the festive period, we head to a little pub that serves craft beer and enjoy sitting by the warmth of the fire, talking and playing board games.

We also put a little money away each month that we use to buy a few edible treats from the local deli and farmers' market. We gather foraged materials to make decorations, and I light the candles on the advent wreath on each Sunday throughout December.

We unplug from internet scrolling, and instead have analogue nights, playing board games and listening to old vinyl records. For us, it's about enjoying the time off together, and stepping back from the rampant consumerism that can make Christmas overwhelming.

I hope this book brings you comfort over a busy season. Embrace JOMO – the joy of missing out – unplug from social media, give yourself permission to rest and take some time out to do some mindful crafting. Enjoy making your own decorations and gifts by hand. Try to avoid spending money you don't have to please others and instead, lean into the simple things that make this season special.

Wishing you a wonderful, peaceful and greener holiday, however you choose to celebrate it.

––––––––

A Seasonal Shift

IT'S IMPORTANT TO TAKE A BREATHER DURING
THIS BUSY PERIOD AND CELEBRATE SEASONAL
RITUALS IN SMALLER, GENTLER WAYS.

Advent Candle Wreath

An advent candle wreath is a lovely, gentle way to count down the weeks till Christmas. Traditionally made with evergreens, it consists of four candles, each one representing the four weeks of advent. One candle is lit on the first Sunday of advent, then two are lit on the second Sunday, three on the third, and finally, all four on the last Sunday. Once they are all lit, it creates a magical feeling, as you sit and admire the shadows cast from the flickering candlelight. Christmas has arrived.

————

You can buy beautiful candle bowls that can be filled with greenery, but it's simple to make an advent wreath yourself using natural materials. I like to use a willow ring for this project, along with some fresh eucalyptus and natural beeswax candles. If you can't get hold of eucalyptus, other evergreen foliage such as holly, ivy or yew work just as well. See page 46 for guidance on how to forage responsibly for evergreens. Once advent is over, you can reuse any greenery to make a garland, or compost it, and retain the willow wreath ring, the candle clips and the floristry wire for future use.

You will need
25cm (10in) willow wreath ring

4 tree candle clips

Large bunch of eucalyptus (I use three different varieties) or evergreen foliage

Floristry wire

4 small or large beeswax taper candles

HOW TO

1. Lay the willow wreath ring flat on a table

2. Space the tree candle clips evenly over the wreath, and clip into place using a willow stem. You may need to manipulate the willow a little with your fingers to be able to attach the clips.

3. Cut the eucalyptus or evergreen foliage into pieces the size of your palm and group the same varieties together.

4. Place two to three stems of eucalyptus or evergreens onto the wreath ring. Using the floristry wire, bind the stems tightly around the ring.

5. Continuing in the same direction, place a second bundle of eucalyptus or foliage on top of the ring. Bind all the stems tightly with the wire, making sure to cover up the wire used to bind the first bunch of greenery.

6. Repeat this process until the ring is filled with greenery. Be mindful of positioning the stems around the candle clips – you don't want any greenery too close to a burning candle.

7. Add the beeswax candles.

Notes
Please be mindful of burning candles next to greenery, and never leave lit candles unattended.

You can also hang this wreath over the dining table. Attach four lengths of twine to the willow ring, making sure they are positioned well away from the candles. Bring the lengths together to form one central knot, and tie tightly. The wreath should be balanced if the twine has been evenly positioned on the ring.

Winter Solstice

December can feel frantic. There are lots of places to be and people to meet, and time can feel like it's slipping away. It's important to take a breather during this busy period and celebrate seasonal rituals in smaller, gentler ways.

————

The Winter Solstice marks the end of autumn (fall) and the beginning of winter. After six months of the days getting shorter and the nights longer, we celebrate the return of the light. In the northern hemisphere, the solstice usually takes place on December 21st or 22nd. Here are some ways to celebrate...

* <u>Fill your home with candlelight</u> to honour the return of the light. Repurpose a brown grocery-store bag into a paper lantern. Simply cut out a few star shapes on each side of the bag, pop in an LED tea light, and place on a windowsill.

* <u>Bring nature indoors.</u> Take a winter walk and gather pine cones, holly or ivy to make wreaths and table decorations. See page 46 for how to make a foraged wreath.

* <u>Watch the beauty of sunrise and sunset.</u> As the day is so short you may be lucky enough to enjoy both.

* <u>Celebrate with a mulled drink.</u> Add a cinnamon stick, a couple of cloves and citrus peels to apple juice in a saucepan. Simmer for 10 minutes to allow the flavours to properly infuse.

* <u>Prepare a feast</u> of comforting foods using seasonal produce, nuts and spices, or bake gingerbread.

* <u>Be still.</u> Recharge over this busy season by taking some time to gaze out the window or sit in nature. Reflect on the past year and let go of anything that no longer serves you. Focus on your intentions for the coming year.

A SEASONAL SHIFT

Christmas Eve

Excitement levels can reach epic proportions on Christmas Eve, so it can be good to encourage kids (and some adults!) to calm down and engage in mindful activities:

————

Embrace the Icelandic tradition of *Jolabokaflod* – the giving and receiving of new books on Christmas Eve. The idea is to sit down in the company of your loved ones, reading and telling stories while enjoying a few chocolate treats and a mug of cocoa.

The books don't have to be brand new – shop for secondhand titles in charity shops, thrift stores and online bookstores. Or do a swap and exchange of books with friends and family.

Turn an old pillowcase into a stocking. Get kids to embellish their own with washable fabric pens. After the big day, the pillowcases can be washed, and then decorated again with new designs the following Christmas. Take a photo of the designs each year so you can look back at the artwork.

If you like to put together Christmas Eve boxes, opt for secondhand items to make them more sustainable. Pyjamas, toys and Christmas storybooks can easily be found in charity shops and thrift stores, or on third-party selling apps. Add a few handmade sweets such as salted caramel fudge (see page 122) or chocolate bark (see page 125).

Sustainable Holiday Ideas

Every year, I used to get a little downhearted at how much rubbish we created from sending Christmas cards and gift giving. From the plastic-covered cards and rolls of wrapping paper, gift tags and sticky tape, to the single-use, plastic-coated gift bags, it all ultimately ended up in landfill. And it's the same for most households. Now, I try to repurpose cards and paper for decorating or wrapping rather than buying new.

————————

If you would like to stop sending cards, have a gentle discussion with friends and family to let them know you won't be participating any more. Send a charity e-card (the charity you normally buy cards from will receive a donation instead), or a text or an email as an alternative festive greeting.

If you like to buy cards, choose ones made from seed paper. You can buy ready-made ones or have a go at making your own. Seed paper is impregnated with wildflower seeds, and once added to compost and watered, the paper biodegrades, and flowers should emerge.

Keep hold of old cards and wrapping paper to repurpose as gift tags. Cut simple square or circle shapes around your favourite part of the design, then punch a hole in the top. Add a piece of jute string, wool or twine. If you are repurposing wrapping paper, reinforce it by sticking the tag onto a piece of cardboard packaging (cereal boxes are ideal) and cutting around it.

Reuse last year's cards to make bunting. Cut triangular shapes out of old cards, then tape the triangles at the widest point to a piece of twine. Hang the bunting with the triangles pointy-side down from a mantelpiece or over a picture.

Greetings card envelopes can be recycled in your cardboard and paper bin but keep hold of the postage stamps and donate them. Lots of charitable organizations accept used stamps and convert them into much needed funds. Using scissors, cut around a stamp, leaving 1cm (about ½ in) of envelope or packaging around it. You then send off the stamps to a charity that participates in this scheme.

When you receive cards or gifts with embellishments, rather than simply recycle them, store them for future use. Collect tissue paper, ribbons, twine or dried flowers and repurpose them for gift wrapping or card making.

Christmas at Home

CHRISTMAS IS WHEN WE WRAP
OURSELVES UP IN NOSTALGIA

Christmas at Home

Our Christmas at home is quiet. We spend Christmas morning enjoying pancakes and sparkling wine for breakfast. We then wrap up warm and head out for a walk by the river, before returning for a light lunch. We might play a board game or watch a movie before eating Christmas dinner in the early evening. Everyone in the household contributes to the meal, whether that's peeling the sprouts or washing the dishes – we do it together.

We see family members on other days over the holidays when we can relax and enjoy one another's company without the pressure of preparing a lavish meal. It wasn't always this way, and we spent years racing from one end of the country to the other for the sake of tradition, but after an honest conversation, we realized that we didn't have a good time and we'd rather do things differently. There is no right or wrong way to do Christmas. There is only your Christmas, so do it your way.

Many of us worry about how to pay for everything when family expectations are high. My advice is to set a budget. This might be for gifts, food or socializing, or possibly all three. Save up throughout the year if you can. Use a banking app to round up any purchases and assign that cash for the holidays. Or why not attempt a no-spend week and pop the money you save from that aside for Christmas? Be clear with family or friends that you have a budget, and you will be sticking to it for gift giving or holiday events. Being open about finances could help everyone feel less stressed over Christmas.

Before the holidays, think about decluttering any areas that look untidy. You don't have to get rid of things – simply putting them away in a cupboard can make a home look and feel better.

Donate or sell decorations you no longer want to keep but be mindful that many charity shops or thrift stores will not want decorations once the holidays are over, so drop them off in good time. Get rid of any broken decorations and check that fairy-light bulbs are all working. Glass baubles cannot be recycled, so if they are irreparable, they must be thrown away. Some plastic decorations can be recycled but check with your local authority for further details.

Get organized. Clean and clear the areas you plan to decorate or rooms that you will be putting guests in. Place warm blankets on guest beds and add a natural candle or a little vase of foraged evergreens to a bedside table. Shop your own home rather than buying new – simply relocating a light or a cushion can make a space feel brand new.

If you have kids, ask them to help you declutter the toys they no longer play with. Donate good-quality books and toys to charity.

Decide what's enough. Set boundaries and give yourself permission to say no to things that don't align with your values. You don't have to accept every invitation or tick off a list of must-dos to enjoy the holidays.

Focus on what brings you joy and take time to rest and recuperate.

Over the next few pages, you'll find some other ways to help you have a simpler and greener Christmas at home.

———

Winter Multipurpose Cleaner

Castile soap is my favourite product to clean with. Originating in Spain, it is made from all-natural vegetable oils (sunflower, hemp, coconut, avocado or olive oil) and free from toxins such as parabens, phthalates, sulphates and petroleum-based products. It's vegan as it contains no animal fats, nor is it tested on animals. It is completely biodegradable and as it can be used for personal hygiene and for cleaning the home, it reduces the need to buy other products, helping to reduce plastic consumption.

———

Liquid Castile soap is readily available from health-food stores and online retailers but check before you buy that nothing has been added to the ingredients list, such as colouring, preservatives or fragrances (other than essential oils). Some brands use palm oil in the making of the soap, so look out for one that is sustainably sourced. As the liquid is extremely concentrated, you only need to use a little for each cleaning job, so a bottle lasts a long time, making it great value for money.

This multipurpose cleaner can be used to clean hobs (stovetops), countertops, appliances, bathtubs and sinks. It's also safe to use Castile soap on stone or marble surfaces as it's alkaline and won't etch the soft stone.

Note that Castile soap can react with the minerals in hard water, which cause the soap to biodegrade and leave behind a white residue on shiny surfaces. This doesn't cause any damage, but you may have to rinse the surface a couple of times to clean off the residue. If you live in a hard-water area, consider using softened or distilled water instead of tap (faucet) water as this will stop the reaction from occurring

Makes one bottle

You will need

1 litre (35fl oz) spray bottle

Tap (faucet) water or softened/distilled water if you live in a hard-water area

3 tbsp liquid Castile soap

Lemon essential oil

Pine needle essential oil

Eucalyptus essential oil

HOW TO

1. Fill the spray bottle with the water until it's approximately 5cm (2in) from the top.

2. Add Castile soap to the bottle (always add the water before the soap, otherwise the mixture goes foamy).

3. Add five drops of lemon essential oil.

4. Add five drops of pine needle essential oil.

5. Add five drops of eucalyptus essential oil.

HOW TO USE

Spray liberally on the surface to be cleaned. Wipe off with a clean cloth.

Notes

Diluting the Castile soap with water means you are also diluting the preservative contained in the soap, which reduces the shelf life of the spray. I find this size of spray bottle lasts two to three weeks before it starts to go off. You will be able to tell as it starts to smell, but I've usually come to the end of the bottle before this happens. Make up a new batch and you are ready to go again.

Pet owners should be aware that many essential oils, including cinnamon and pine, are not safe to use around pets. Always speak to your veterinarian before using any essential oils in the home. Pregnant women should also discuss the use of essential oils with their midwife or healthcare advisor.

Scenting the Home Naturally

If lingering odours from cooking have you reaching for an air freshener, consider the impact this has on the environment and your wellbeing before you use it. The majority of air fresheners are manufactured abroad and shipped halfway around the world. Many are made from plastic derived from petroleum and need vast amounts of energy and water to produce. Most air fresheners release volatile organic compounds (VOCs) into the air in your home and can cause respiratory problems, headaches, allergies and asthma. They are also particularly harmful to pets, which can ingest pollutant particles that have settled on their fur when they groom themselves. The good news is there are other ways to scent your home that are safe and better for the planet.

————

Winter herb bundle

I grow a lot of fresh herbs in the garden. Some are for use in cooking, others for feeding pollinators, but I grow most purely for their wonderful scents. At the end of the growing season, I like to cut and dry them in bunches, along with a few flowers such as alliums, hydrangeas and yarrow. Hung over a window or strung on a mantelpiece, they not only look beautiful but also retain their intoxicating aromas. At Christmastime, I like to bundle them together and decorate them with a little velvet ribbon. They are good popped in cupboards and wardrobes, as they have the added benefit of repelling insects and dust mites.

Makes one bundle
You will need
Bunches of sage, rosemary and thyme
Scissors
Twine (hemp, jute or sisal are the eco-friendliest)

HOW TO

1. Cut the stems of each herb bunch to your chosen length. Strip away any of the lower leaves where you plan to tie the bundle. If you don't remove the lower leaves from the stems before you bind them with twine, the herbs can become mouldy and affect the rest of the bundle.

2. Cut a 30cm (12in) length of twine for each herb bundle. Wrap the twine tightly around the stem of each bundle and secure with a tight knot, leaving one end of the twine long enough to attach to a hook or peg rail.

3. Hang the bundle upside down. Squeeze the herbs occasionally to help release their wonderful scent.

Natural air freshener

This is perfect to use in bathrooms where a little extra aroma busting may be required!

<u>HOW TO</u>

1. Add bicarbonate of soda (baking soda) to a depth of around 4cm (1½in) in a glass jar, then sprinkle in a few drops of your favourite festive scented essential oil* (try cloves, cinnamon, nutmeg, orange, pine etc.). Punch a couple of holes in the jar lid and screw it on. Once the smell begins to fade, simply add a few more drops of oil.

Scented pine cones

The ideal time to forage for pine cones is autumn (fall). Take a reusable produce bag and head out to the park or the woods. Never pick any pine cones from a tree but check under conifers for those that have dropped to the ground. When foraging for natural materials, it's essential to check out the legal position for the area you live in as you may require permission from the local authority or landowner.

<u>HOW TO</u>

1. Soak the pine cones in cold water, rinse, then place them on a baking sheet lined with foil. Pop in the oven at 180°C/350°F/gas mark 4 and bake for 30–60 minutes. Keep an eye on them to make sure they don't burn. Remove the baking sheet from the oven and allow the pine cones to cool. Place them in a large sealable bag and add a few drops of essential oils* – cloves, cinnamon, nutmeg, orange, or pine all work well. Seal the bag, then shake and leave for several days. Add more drops of oil if you need a stronger scent.

2. Remove the cones from the bag and display in a wooden bowl or make a rustic garland of pine cones strung on natural twine.

*See note on pets and essential oils, page 29.

Reed Diffuser

A simple and effective way to scent your home at Christmas is to make your own reed diffuser using essential oils. Popped on a shelf, mantelpiece or bedside table, these diffusers can be safely left to release a gentle fragrance over time.

————

Wherever possible, buy pure organic essential oils to guarantee that the plants used to make them were not sprayed with herbicides or pesticides as these can pass into the oils during the steam distillation process. It is also better to buy from companies that use native plants and share their origins on their labels.

Use whichever essential oils you like for your diffuser. Choose one oil on its own or create a blend. To get you in the festive spirit, try adding a few drops of sweet orange, cinnamon, cloves, fir, nutmeg or pine essential oils.

This recipe makes one bottle to scent a small room. If you have a larger room, use a bigger bottle and double the quantities of the ingredients.

You will need
1 small glass bottle with a narrow neck

7½ tbsp sweet almond oil

30 drops essential oil* (if using a blend, divide by the number of oils you are using, e.g. 15 sweet orange, 15 pine)

Scissors

3–5 bamboo skewers (or use natural fibre diffuser reeds)

HOW TO

1. Wash the bottle in warm, soapy water.

2. Rinse, then leave to air dry.

3. Pour the sweet almond oil into the bottle.

4. Add 30 drops of your chosen essential oil(s).

5. Using the scissors, remove the pointy end from each bamboo skewer.

6. Insert one bamboo skewer into the bottle and stir to combine.

7. Pop the remaining skewers into the bottle and leave for several hours.

8. Lift all three skewers out, turn them upside down and place the unscented ends into the bottle, leaving the scented ends on display.

9. Repeat this last step every two to three days.

10. Refresh the oil and essential oils once a month.

*See note on pets and essential oils, page 29.

Candlelight

Candles help make a home feel relaxed and cozy. They create a comforting atmosphere and provide a natural warmth, which is good for lifting our spirits in the depths of winter.

———

Some candles, however, are better for us than others. Most candles found in retail stores are made from paraffin wax (also known as mineral wax). A petroleum waste product, paraffin is bleached, synthetically coloured and fragranced. When it's burning, fumes released are comparable with those from a diesel engine and are especially harmful to anyone who suffers with asthma and other respiratory problems. Paraffin wax candles also produce a lot of smoke and can leave soot residue on the walls.

I use candles made with beeswax, rapeseed (canola) or soy wax, which are non-toxic, sustainable and smoke free. Beeswax gives off a delicate honey scent and is a natural air purifier. Both soy and rapeseed (canola) wax are suitable for vegans, but it is important to look for responsibly sourced and non-GMO products. If you are a fan of scented candles, choose ones made with sustainable plant waxes and fragranced with pure essential oils.

White dinner candles and tea lights made in a sustainable way can be harder to find, but they are available in some stores and online. Look for the list of ingredients for each candle to confirm their eco credentials.

These are some of my favourite ways to display candles over Christmas and wintertime:

Recycle clear glass wine or cordial bottles. Wash and remove the labels. Boil the kettle, allow the water to cool, then fill the bottles about two-thirds full. Add a sprig of greenery to each bottle – fresh herbs such as thyme, rosemary or eucalyptus all look stunning displayed this way. Using boiled water helps to stop discolouration occurring in the bottle. Add your plants to the bottle by pushing them in gently with the handle of a long wooden spoon. Top with a dinner candle. If the candle is too big to fit properly, shave a little off the bottom of the candle with a knife until it fits tightly.

Alternatively, you can find candle holders that simply slot into the top of the bottle. These bottles also look nice without water and filled with dried grasses or flowers.

Pop a sustainable wax tea light in a glass holder and line the rim with sprigs of evergreen rosemary. Attach with some jute twine tied in a bow. Recycled glass yoghurt pots and jam (jelly) jars work well for this purpose.

Invest in a wall sconce to bring some additional cozy light to a room. You can find beautiful vintage pieces in brass and copper. Check out the hashtag #vintagesconce on Instagram to find quirky pieces and search third-party selling apps, vintage fairs and thrift stores.

Tip

If you are a fan of wax melts, be aware that many of these are also made with paraffin wax, so look for non-toxic and eco-friendly waxes instead.

Deck
the
Halls

MY HOUSE IS CALM,
CONSIDERED AND MOST
IMPORTANT OF ALL, SIMPLE.

Deck the Halls

A single strand of fairy lights woven round a window frame, a few windfall branches strung with dried orange slices, the golden glow of a beeswax candle, Christmas decorating doesn't need to be complicated or expensive.

Every year, retailers pile their shelves high with new decorations, urging you to consume more. It can be difficult not to splurge and add a new item to your collection, but before you buy, consider what a decoration is made from. Most mass-produced baubles and tinsel are produced overseas using non-recyclable plastics and need vast amounts of energy for production and transportation. Many are coated in glitter that contains microplastics, which pollute water sources and harm marine life. These decorations are not widely recyclable, and when they come to the end of their lifespan, they end up in landfill where they leach toxins into the environment.

If you are buying new decorations, look for ones made with sustainable materials such as glass, metal, lokta paper and wood. For tinsel fans you can find sustainable alternatives made from recycled paper and copper wire. Search online for eco-friendly tinsel. Don't forget to shop secondhand and look for decorations in charity shops and vintage stores.

The most sustainable decorations are of course the ones you already own. Looking after them is key, keeping them free from dust and dirt, before securing them in tissue paper or bubble wrap when storing them away for next year.

I like to use natural materials for decorating. Whenever I'm out walking, I try to observe the plants and flowers that line the hedgerows and the riverbank. It's a mindful activity that you can do throughout the year as it requires you to slow down and pay attention. I look for evergreens and grasses, perennials that I know will produce beautiful seedheads, and I make a note of their location on my phone, so I know where to return to. I've found most of my foraged materials this way, from the overgrown ivy that pushes its tendrils through the railings on a piece of waste ground and the tree that drops pinecones onto the pavement at the side of the golf course, to the small patch of Queen Anne's Lace that sits on the edge of the riverbank, I cut only what I need and will use.

Dried flowers are ideal to use in winter displays. Poppy seed heads, teasels, thistles and grasses are lovely added to wreaths or popped in a vase. Please avoid buying from commercial suppliers as the flowers will most likely have been treated with anti-mould chemicals, hardened, bleached or synthetically dyed. Naturally dried flowers should last for a couple of years and can be added to the compost bin at the end of their lifespan. Those that have been chemically treated, however, will have to be sent to landfill.

If you like to buy fresh flowers at Christmas, then there are a few points to consider. Supermarkets and garden centres sell red and pink poinsettia plants, but these have been industrially grown and forced in heated glass houses. They also usually die during the festivities and are then thrown away along with the plastic pot. Flowers or other natural materials that have been spray painted or had glitter added should also be avoided as these are effectively plastics and will have to be sent to landfill. For a simpler festive arrangement, fill a vase or a jug with a bunch of locally sourced fresh eucalyptus and berries which you can find in independent florists. The berries can be composted once they are past their best, whilst the eucalyptus can be utilized in dried flower arrangements or turned into pot pourri.

There are lots of easy ways to make our homes feel more festive by using up bits and pieces you already have in the cupboard. If you knit or crochet, turn those odds and ends of wool into hanging garlands or tree ornaments.

Get the kids involved and make pom-poms from leftover scraps of yarn or paper chains using strips of newspaper, comic books or wallpaper samples. You can find video tutorials for these on YouTube.

Aim to make your decorations low waste using recycled and natural materials. A garland made from popcorn and cranberries strung over the mantelpiece looks beautiful, whilst dried orange peel cut into star shapes is great for adding to wreaths. From the larder, create salt dough decorations or bake gingerbread cookies to hang on the tree. A few pieces of recycled card, wallpaper samples or brown paper bags from the grocery store can be turned

into hanging stars to display in a window. Get outdoors and pick up a few small sticks to create snowflake shapes. Bind the sticks together with floristry wire and tie jute twine on to make a hanging loop. You could also make a larger star shape and wind a string of battery-operated fairy lights around the sticks to display on a mantelpiece or sideboard.

Over the next few pages, you'll see how I decorate for Christmas. I use mostly natural, sustainable and recycled materials, and along with a few vintage items I've collected and some pieces I have made myself. My house is calm, considered and most important of all, simple.

———

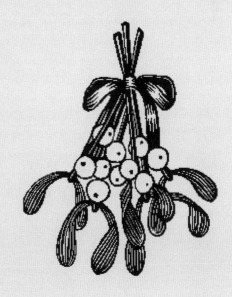

Christmas Trees

Putting the Christmas tree up in December is always an occasion to be celebrated. It's when the magic of the season really begins for many. But, overall, Christmas trees are not very environmentally friendly. An artificial tree is made with petroleum plastic (PVC) and shipped from overseas. And, although it will last for many years, once the tree comes to the end of its lifespan, it will end up in landfill and take hundreds of years to break down. If you are buying an artificial tree, opt for a secondhand one, and if you are replacing one, donate it to charity or sell it on.

―――――――

When grown correctly, real Christmas trees are renewable resources that benefit nature and support biodiversity. It takes eight to 10 years for a tree to reach around six feet (1.8m) tall, and during this time it absorbs carbon. Search online for a local Christmas tree farm, and when visiting, ask questions about how its trees are grown, looked after and felled. Many will let you go into the field and pick your own tree before cutting it down in front of you. Supporting local businesses benefits your community and cuts down on transport too.

If you buy a real tree that was possibly felled a while ago, treat it like a bunch of flowers. Saw a little off the trunk to allow the tree to absorb water (you don't need to do this with a freshly cut tree). Position it well away from radiators, as the heat can dry it out. Make sure the base of the trunk is always in a bowl of fresh water but look out for curious pets. Sweep up any needles and add them to your compost bin.

You also need to consider what to do with a real tree after the holidays. If you have space in the garden, leave it to rot down in a shady, dry spot. Or chop it into smaller pieces and stack the branches together to provide wildlife with shelter. Alternatively, check if your local authority offers a composting service, or arrange to have it chipped by a tree surgeon and use it as mulch for garden pathways. Local goat farmers may also take your old Christmas tree as goats love to feast on them.

A tree that has been grown in a container is a great sustainable option. These trees are kept indoors over the holiday period, then placed outside until the following year. They are ideal for smaller spaces, but the tree will need repotting into a larger container every couple of years to ensure it stays healthy and you will have to remember to water it well during dry spells. You can then bring the tree back into your home the following Christmas.

There are also places that rent a tree in a pot for the duration of the Christmas holiday. My local farm shop has recently introduced this service and although numbers of trees are limited, I'm hopeful to make the list this year. Of course, the most sustainable option is to not have a tree at all. It is easy to make an alternative using natural or repurposed materials. Twigs, wooden offcuts, books or an old set of step ladders look fantastic when decorated with a strand of fairy lights and a few baubles. Indoor plants can also look festive adorned with fairy lights and are perfect for small spaces.

Foraged Wreath

Making a wreath is a lovely way to slow down and embrace the season. It is a truly mindful activity, and one that helps you to pause and take a breather during this busy and often demanding time of the year.

———————

I forage for natural materials from my garden and in the hedgerows to use in my wreaths. I ensure anything I cut has as little impact on the local environment as possible. This means I only take what I need in areas where plants are in abundance, and I leave plenty behind for birds and other wildlife. When foraging for natural materials, it's essential to check out the legal situation in the area you live as you may require permission from the local authority or landowner.

I also add a little extra greenery to the foraged materials I've gathered, including eucalyptus from the florist, offcuts from the Christmas tree and flower heads that I've cut and dried over previous seasons.

I like to use a straw ring as a base as it gives the wreath a lovely shape and once the materials are secured in place they don't tend to fall out. The rings are biodegradable and you can add them to the compost bin, but if allowed to dry out, I find they can be used the following year. Straw rings come in various sizes, and you can easily find them online.

Plant materials for a wreath

* <u>Evergreens</u>: Pine, eucalyptus, spruce, fir, yew, leylandii, ivy (including the flower heads)

* <u>Berries</u>: Holly, cotoneaster, rosehips

* <u>Dried Flowers</u>: Old man's beard (wild clematis), grasses, hydrangea, wild carrot, teasels, honesty, poppies, thistles, weeds!

continues overleaf...

Selection of foraged evergreens, berries, dried seedheads and grasses

Secateurs

Straw ring – I use a 30cm (12in) size

Roll of floristry wire

Mossing pins

Ribbon

Twine

HOW TO

1. Shake the foraged materials gently to remove any hidden insects.

2. Sort into piles of the same plant or flower.

3. Cut any evergreen materials into pieces around the size of the palm of your hand.

4. On the flat side of the straw ring, insert the end of the floristry wire into the straw, pushing it in to a depth of 1–2cm (about ½–¾in).

5. With the curved side of the straw ring pointing towards your body, hold the ring in one hand and with the other, pull the floristry wire under the ring and over tightly, repeating this action several times until the wire feels secure.

6. To form a neat shape with a wreath, work in an anti-clockwise direction and add materials onto the part of the ring that's closest to your body.

7. Select two to three pieces of foliage and place them on the curved side of the straw ring. Using the floristry wire, bind the pieces together by pulling the wire under the ring and over the stems tightly, repeating this action until the foliage feels secure. You want to ensure that the straw ring is hidden beneath the foliage, so you may need additional pieces of foliage to cover any gaps. As before, bind the stem tightly with the floristry wire.

8. Next, select another small bunch of foliage. Place this on top of the ring. Add a stem of dried flowers, seedheads or berries. Bind all the stems tightly with the wire, making sure to cover up the wire used to bind the first bunch of foliage.

9. Repeat this process until the straw ring is filled with greenery. After you have added the final pieces of foliage, turn the straw ring over and cut the floristry wire. Thread any excess wire under the previous strands and push the end of it into the straw to secure firmly.

10. If you have any gaps on the inside or outside of the ring, use the mossing pins to add pieces of evergreen material. Simply push the pin through the stem of the foliage and into the straw ring to fix. The mossing pins can also be used to attach pine cones, dried orange slices, cinnamon sticks and other materials if you choose to add these to your design.

11. I like to add a velvet ribbon to my wreath, which I tie in a bow and use a mossing pin to fix in place. To hang the wreath, I thread twine through the binding wire on the flat side of the ring and tie it together in a knot.

12. If you are hanging the wreath outdoors, be mindful that natural foliage can dry out. Rain will usually keep your wreath looking fresh, but if the weather is dry and bright, you may wish to spray the foliage with a little water.

13. After the holidays, remove the foliage and add it to the compost bin. Retain any mossing pins and floristry wire to reuse the following year. Allow the straw ring to dry thoroughly, and then store for next Christmas.

Table Settings

I like to keep my Christmas dinner table simple and natural. For me, it's all about the eating rather than the styling, but I do think it's nice to add a little greenery and light a few candles to make things feel more festive. I don't believe in keeping things for best, and everything I use at the table is loved and utilized all year round.

———————

Candleholders. A few ideas for Christmas table candles:

* Use clear glass wine or cordial bottles and turn them into candlesticks. See page 38 for the how-to. These look beautiful filled with red berries or some herbs cut from the garden.

* I like to add something shiny to the Christmas dinner table. Search in vintage shops, thrift stores, at fairs, on vintage apps and online for brass or copper candlesticks. Tie a velvet ribbon around the top to make them more festive.

* Pop a beeswax or rapeseed (canola) tea light in a glass holder and line the rim with sprigs of evergreen rosemary. Attach with some jute twine tied in a bow. I like to use glass yoghurt pots for this.

* Small terracotta pots filled with dinner candles look beautiful too. Put the candle in the pot and weigh it down with small pebbles to hold it in position. Arrange a few sprigs of fir or rosemary on top to disguise the pebbles.

Vintage stoneware ink bottles. I love using these to decorate my table at any time of the year. They can be used as small bud vases and are perfect to hold a little greenery for Christmas. They also come in handy as candle holders. You can find them in all different sizes and designs, and vintage stores and fairs usually have them in stock as they are popular and relatively inexpensive.

Table linen. One of the best ways to be greener at home is to switch from artificial fibres to natural ones. At Christmastime, stores are full of homeware products such as tablecloths, aprons and napkins made from synthetic materials. Artificial fibres are cheaper and easier to produce than natural fibres, but they are derived from petrochemicals, require a lot of energy to manufacture, are not biodegradable and ultimately end up in landfill.

Choosing natural fibres helps to support employment and the economies of developing nations as they are mostly grown and harvested there. Natural fibres are also biodegradable, compostable and easily recyclable. Look for tablecloths and napkins made of linen or organic cotton. If you are shopping for secondhand linen, check out third-party apps, vintage fairs, charity shops and thrift stores. Alternatively, use a bed sheet as a makeshift tablecloth – no one will know!

continues overleaf...

Napkins. At each place setting, roll up a napkin and tie a length of jute twine around it, with the bow pointing upwards. Tuck some natural elements into the twine – a sprig of eucalyptus, rosemary, rosehips, a cinnamon stick, a dried orange slice, a mini pine cone or a dried poppy seed stem.

Mix and match. It doesn't matter if you don't have matching crockery, cutlery, glasses or table linen. Put out your favourite things as these will bring you the greatest pleasure, and there is something special about seeing these items being used and loved.

Foraged or natural materials. Try using dried hydrangea flowers and seedheads in small bud vases; creating a garland of foraged holly and ivy to run the length of the table; placing a bowl of pine cones or acorns in the centre of the table; or putting a clementine with its leaves attached or cut-open pomegranate on a small plate at each place setting.

Christmas Crackers

Invented by London confectioner Tom Smith, crackers have adorned the Christmas dinner table since Victorian times. They began life as sugared almonds wrapped in tissue paper with a love note added and were designed for gentlemen to give to ladies as small tokens of their affection. Over time, Smith developed the cracker into what we know it as today, a tube that goes bang when pulled, and filled with a paper party hat, a joke and a novelty item. Of course, Smith's crackers were all made by hand, as were the contents, unlike the crackers found in most retailers these days.

———————

Christmas crackers are usually produced overseas, and take a vast amount of energy to produce before they are shipped and transported to stores. Lots are filled with plastic novelties that are immediately discarded after the cracker has been pulled and sent to landfill. That's a huge carbon footprint all for the sake of a paper hat. If you like buying crackers for your Christmas dinner table, look for eco-friendly reusable ones, those you fill yourself, or plastic-free and recyclable options.

It's nice to welcome friends and family with a little gift at the Christmas dinner table, but it's not necessary to create so much waste for the sake of 'tradition'. Instead, I like to make my own low-waste crackers from repurposing packaging. These crackers won't go bang as I don't add a cracker snap, but they do include a small, personal gift for my guests that they will hopefully appreciate and value.

I find packaging that contained books or envelopes with strong cardboard backing works well for this DIY, so I keep hold of these whenever I receive them in the mail.

continues overleaf...

Makes one cracker

You will need

Ruler

Piece of cardboard around 14 x 18cm (5½ x 7in)

Pencil

Cutting mat/magazines/newspaper

Scissors

Washi/paper tape

Treats (see below for ideas)

1 fabric napkin or piece of fabric, around
40 x 40cm (16 x 16in)

2 pieces of velvet ribbon, cut into
50cm (20in) strips

Ideas for gifts inside crackers

* For children: Reusable party hats (search
  online for tutorials on how to make your
  own), crayons and erasers, character toys
  (car-boot and jumble sales are brilliant
  places to find these secondhand), lollipops.

* For adults: Mini pots of blackberry and bay
  leaf jam (see recipe page 118), mini pots of
  honey or marmalade, packets of wildflower
  seeds, lip balm (see how to make your own
  on page 86), citrus gin miniature (see page
  115), lottery ticket, small beeswax candles.

* Everyone: Handwritten jokes, festive fact,
  chocolate coins.

HOW TO

1. Using the ruler, measure along the longest
   side of the card and mark each 3.5cm (1⅜in)
   point with a pencil.

2. Repeat along the bottom of the longest side
   of the card.

3. Join the marks on the top and the bottom
   of the card together with a ruler.

4. Place the card on a cutting mat or a couple
   of magazines/newspapers.

5. Using the scissors, score along each line
   to make the cardboard flexible enough to
   bend into shape.

6. Fold the cardboard into a tube shape and
   fix with a piece of washi/paper tape.

7. Fill the cracker with your chosen treats.

8. Lay out your napkin or piece of fabric, then
   place the cardboard tube in the centre.

9. Wrap the napkin or piece of fabric around
   the cracker.

10. Twist the ends of the cracker and tie a
    bow around each end with a piece of
    the velvet ribbon.

11. After the crackers have been unwrapped,
    retain the napkins and velvet ribbons to
    use again. The cardboard packaging can
    be recycled, or if it's still usable, keep for
    next Christmas.

Flower Frog

A flower frog is a piece of equipment used in floral design. It is generally made of metal and placed inside a vase or bowl, where it holds the flowers in place. If you like arranging flowers and get annoyed when they flop over, it's worth investing in a flower frog. You can find secondhand ones made of glass, ceramic and metal. Search for them at vintage fairs or online. If using a flower frog in a vase or bowl, make sure it can be submerged in water and won't go rusty.

———————

I like to make flower frogs from recycled materials, and I've converted plastic yoghurt pots and lids for this purpose before. You simply poke several holes in the lid, then reattach it to the pot. Fill the pot with water and push the stems of the flowers through the lid. Disguise the yoghurt pot in a ceramic vase or jug. The yoghurt pot flower frog is great for holding bunches of daffodils, tulips or hyacinths in spring, as these all have a tendency to fall over. Don't forget that the water will still need changing every few days.

You can also make a more permanent flower frog out of air-drying clay. However, as the clay is not fired in a kiln it can't be submerged in water. This flower frog sits handily on top of a jam (jelly) jar, and works well for fresh flowers, but I find it particularly useful for dried arrangements of seedheads and grasses.

There is no set size for this DIY flower frog. Use whatever size jam jar you have at hand. I have an old French vintage jar that I like as it's wider than a regular supermarket-size jar and I can fill it with more flowers, but any jar will do.

You will need

1 ball white air-drying clay

Wooden board or crafting mat

Rolling pin

Jam (jelly) jar (without the lid, washed and dried)

Small knife

Clay crafting tools or metal teaspoon

Scissors

continues overleaf...

HOW TO

1. Place the ball of clay onto the wooden board or crafting mat.

2. Using the palm of your hand, push down firmly on the clay to flatten.

3. Using the rolling pin, roll the clay out to form a wide circle approximately 1cm (½in) thick.

4. Place the jam jar open side down onto the clay, then using either a knife or one of the crafting tools, draw/mark all the way around the jar.

5. Using scissors, cut around the mark until you have a circle shape.

6. The circle may look a little rough around the edges, but you can smooth this down with a finger, or if the clay feels a little dry, use a bit of water.

7. Place the circle of clay back down on the board and using either a crafting tool or the handle end of a metal teaspoon, push through the clay to form a hole.

8. Repeat this action until you have several holes in the clay. The holes don't need to be in specific places –you can space them out however you like.

9. Lift the circle of clay and place it on top of the jam jar.

10. You may find that the holes haven't penetrated all the way through the clay, so push through them once again with the tool or spoon.

11. Tidy up any rough edges and remove any debris.

12. Leave the circle of clay to harden, which should take around three days.

13. Once the clay is fully hard, place the circle on top of the jam jar and poke dried flower stems through the holes to finish.

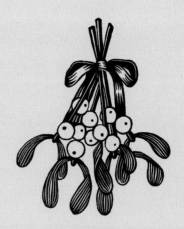

Star Garland

This garland is one of my favourite things to make using recycled materials, and who would ever believe it was made from old tomato-purée (paste) tubes? We seem to go through a lot of these tubes in our house, and I always try to retain some to make more decorations for Christmas. As well as tomato-purée tubes, you can use pâté, cheese or hand-cream metal tubes for this crafting project.

———————

I like to use paper-covered wire for this garland as it's easy to bend and shape as well as durable. You can find paper-covered wire in craft stores or online. Alternatively, you can use floristry wire or twine.

You will need
3 old tomato-purée (paste) tubes
Scissors
Spoon
Dish towel or magazine
Star-shaped punch cutter and/or star template
Pencil
Paper-covered wire
Washi tape

HOW TO

1. Cut off both ends of the purée tubes with scissors. Add the plastic cap to the recycling bin.

2. Cut along one side of the tube lengthways, from top to bottom. Please be mindful of sharp edges when cutting the metal tubes.

3. Open the flattened tube, then using a spoon, scrape off any remaining purée (which you can store in the fridge and use later for cooking).

4. Wash the flattened tube in warm, soapy water, and dry.

5. Place the flattened tube gold-side down onto a dish towel or magazine.

6. Using the back of a spoon, push gently down on the metal to smooth out any creases or bumps.

7. Use the cutting punch on the metal to create small star shapes.

8. If you are using a star template, place it on the printed side of the flattened tube and draw around it with a pencil. When you turn over the tube, you'll see the impression of the star is left on the gold side. Cut out the star shape.

9. Attach the back of the stars to the paper-covered wire with tape. I like to attach one large star surrounded by two smaller-sized stars and then repeat the pattern until the garland is complete.

10. If you prefer to make hanging ornaments instead of a garland, follow the instructions as above, but instead of fixing to the paper-covered wire, poke a small hole through the top of each star and attach a piece of thread. You can also glue the stars back-to-back to conceal the printed packaging from view.

Snowflake Decoration

This is a great activity to do with kids in the run-up to Christmas and a brilliant way to teach them about recycling and resources. I've shared the how-to for one simple design, but you can get creative and position the tube pieces in lots of different ways.

———

You will need
Ruler
3–4 toilet-roll tubes
Pencil
Scissors
Glue stick or glue dots (for an eco-friendly option, search online for natural glue)
Clothes pegs/small craft pegs
Twine

HOW TO

1. Using the ruler, measure 1cm (½in) along the length of one toilet tube and mark with a pencil. Repeat this along the tube, marking each 1cm (½in) increment. Rotate the tube slightly and repeat to make a second set of marks, then line the two marks up with the ruler and draw a connecting line.

2. Using scissors, cut along each line until you have small circles of tube.

3. Position five pieces of tube to form a flower shape (see photograph).

4. Dot a small bit of glue near the bottom of one of the pieces of tube and attach it to another piece of tube. You can also use two glue dots for this task. Use a clothes peg/craft peg to hold the pieces together until the glue sets.

5. Repeat with the remaining pieces of tube until the flower shape is fully formed and secure.

6. Bend each of the remaining pieces of tube in half to form a small 'v' shape.

7. To attach the 'v' shapes to the main body of the snowflake, dot a little bit of glue or a glue dot on the bottom of one of the already attached pieces of tube and the same on the one directly opposite. Position the 'v' shape point side down and attach the two wider sides of the 'v' to the glue. Again, use a clothes/craft peg to secure.

8. Cut a piece of twine and feed it through the top of one of the larger pieces of tube, and gently tie a knot to secure.

9. Hang the snowflakes from Christmas tree branches, or in a window where everyone will be able to admire your handiwork.

Natural Garland

I used to make this natural garland to grace the lovely reclaimed black-iron fireplace we had in our old house. It was something I looked forward to creating every year – the scent from the eucalyptus was glorious throughout the festive season, and I loved the orange slices dangling from the mantelpiece. Our new home doesn't have a fireplace, but I still like to make this garland as part of my winter celebrations. It looks impressive tied to the banister on the staircase, and I can smell the woody, fresh scent of the eucalyptus when I pass by.

———————

I've included instructions for both mantelpiece and banister. But you could use it to cover the top of a cabinet, a shelf or a windowsill as this simple, natural garland looks good anywhere.

TO DRY ORANGE SLICES

You will need

3 large oranges

Knife

Chopping board

Baking sheet

Baking/parchment paper

Scissors

Jute twine

HOW TO

1. Preheat the oven to 60°C/140°F/ the lowest setting for a gas oven.

2. Wash and dry the oranges.

3. Cut each orange into approximately 1cm (½in) slices.

4. Cover the baking sheet with a piece of baking/parchment paper. Lay each slice on top of the paper.

5. Using a small knife or scissors, make a small incision just below the rind on each slice (this is where you will attach the twine once they come out of the oven).

6. Pop in the oven for around four hours, turning the slices once every hour.

7. If they still feel sticky or a little wet after the four hours are up, don't worry, they will continue to dry in the air.

8. Once the slices are cool, attach pieces of jute twine and hang.

continues overleaf...

TO MAKE THE GARLAND

You will need

Jute twine

Scissors

Washi tape/paper tape

Secateurs

Eucalyptus stems

Floristry wire

Dried orange slices

Tip

After Christmas, pop the eucalyptus stems and orange slices in the compost bin, recycle the paper tape, reuse the jute twine in the garden (or reserve for next year) and retain the floristry wire for other crafting projects.

HOW TO

1. Cut a piece of twine the length of the mantelpiece or banister.

2. Pop a piece of washi/paper tape onto each end of the twine and attach it to the mantelpiece or banister.

3. Using the secateurs, trim the eucalyptus stems into similar-sized pieces.

4. Cut a few 10cm (4in) lengths of floristry wire and set aside.

5. Select two pieces of eucalyptus and, using a piece of the floristry wire, bind the bottom of the two stems together tightly.

6. Tuck these stems under the jute twine, then bind the stems and the twine together with more pieces of floristry wire.

7. Repeat this method until you have filled the twine up with foliage.

8. You may need to hold up the jute twine with additional pieces of tape as the weight of the stems may pull it down.

9. Tie the dried orange slices onto the twine at regular intervals until you have a pleasing, even display.

Considered
Gifting

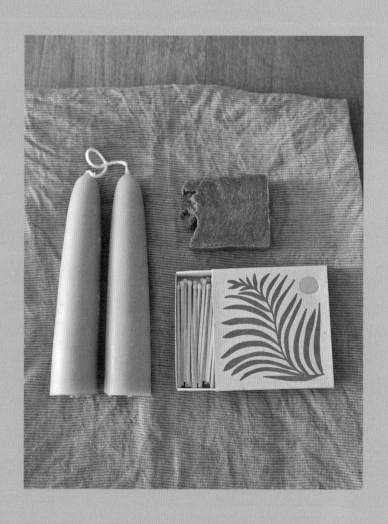

A HOMEMADE GIFT IS A LOVELY
WAY TO SHOW SOMEONE YOU
ARE THINKING OF THEM.

Considered Gifting

I love Christmas – the food, the decorations, movies both good and bad, and most of all being with my family. What I really don't like is overconsumption, buying things we don't really like or need, the enormous amount of waste and the greed of so many. Adopting a more ethical approach means shopping is more enjoyable and we can give something truly unique to the people we care about.

When it comes to gift giving, think about the five guiding principles - refuse, reduce, reuse, recycle and rot. First, refuse to buy products that will ultimately end up in landfill and reduce by buying only what you need rather than making impulse purchases. Ask yourself if you can reuse or recycle an item rather than buying new and can it rot, i.e., is it biodegradable or compostable?

To ease yourself into a more sustainable Christmas, why not make a commitment to choose a secondhand gift or make a gift for every new one you buy. A homemade gift is a lovely way to show someone you are thinking of them.

Every year, we bake six Christmas cakes for members of our family (see page 111 for the recipe). We've been doing this for over 15 years as an alternative to buying gifts. Everyone in the family appreciates receiving the cake and they are often disappointed when they finish eating it so quickly! It wasn't always this way. Previously we bought lots of things we didn't need or want and after Christmas, these gifts were consigned to the back of a cupboard or handed into the charity shop. Eventually we realized that we didn't want to participate in this any more, so we had a conversation with our family to let them know our feelings. Thankfully, they all agreed, and now we just buy gifts for the children. Shopping for gifts can be overwhelming and stressful, and it's a relief not to have to do it any more.

For those of you feeling the same way, chances are your friends and family do too. Be brave and let others know your concerns. Or why not consider introducing a 'Secret Santa' arrangement? This way everyone puts their name into a hat, draws one name out, and each person gives and receives one gift. It can be far easier to think of one meaningful gift than lots of impersonal ones. You could set a theme, so everyone participating makes a gift, or buys a book or vouchers for use at a local business.

If you are gift shopping, aim to support local, independent businesses. Supporting a local store benefits the rest of the community. Businesses stay open, grow, employ local people and pass on traditional skills. Local businesses use the services of other local businesses for printing, accounts, design and maintenance, which helps to strengthen the entire community.

A homemade gift is a lovely way to show someone you are thinking of them. My mum is a wonderful knitter and has produced

beautiful mittens and jumpers over the
years. I'm lucky enough to be the recipient
of many of these gifts, and I know she puts
a lot of thought and care into each item.
Making things by hand takes time and skill
and can be extremely rewarding. Throughout
this chapter, you'll find ideas for simple gifts
you can create at home. They are all budget
friendly, sustainable and will be very
satisfying to make.

Don't forget about others less fortunate
at Christmas too. Donate to charity, buy
toys for kids who might not get a gift
at Christmas, contribute to your local
foodbank, or donate blankets and food
to animal shelters.

––––––––

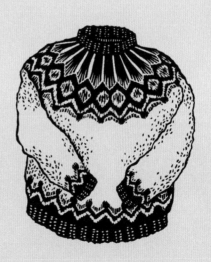

Greetings-card gift box

Repurpose packaging or old greetings cards to make gift boxes. Board-back envelopes or book mailers are ideal for making larger-sized boxes, whereas rectangular or square cards are better for small ones. These gift boxes are lovely filled with a bar of lavender, peppermint and rosemary soap (see page 84), a 'no-sew' herb sachet (see page 88), or lip balm (see page 86).

———

You will need

A piece of cardboard packaging or an old greetings card

Scissors

Ruler

Pencil

Paper tape or washi tape

Twine, string or ribbon (optional)

Note

The instructions opposite are for making a box using rectangular cards and packaging. If you are using a square card, there will be no long or short sides, so choose any two opposite sides to cut and fold as required.

HOW TO

1. Fold the cardboard packaging in half if using. If you are repurposing a card, the fold is there already.

2. Using scissors, cut along the folded edge of the card, giving you two rectangles or squares.

3. If you are using a greetings card, make sure that the design is facing downwards as this will be the top of the gift box. If using packaging, use the blank side as the top, leaving any address labels on the inside.

4. Take the ruler and draw a diagonal line from one corner of the packaging/card to the other. Repeat on the remaining corner. The two lines should cross in the middle, and this is your marker for folding.

5. Fold one side of the packaging/card until it meets the cross in the middle. Repeat on the opposite side.

6. Open the card back up and fold the other two sides into the middle as before.

7. Open the card again and, using scissors, cut along the folded lines on both shorter sides of the packaging/card until you reach the line. You should have no cuts on the longer sides of the packaging/card.

8. Fold the long sides up and bend the shorter ends in towards one another. Pull the remaining ends up and over the shorter ends, and secure with washi or paper tape.

9. To make the bottom of the box, cut approximately ½ cm (¼ in) off each side of the packaging/card. Repeat the previous six steps again to complete the gift box.

Gift Wrapping

I like to wrap gifts with fabric using the Japanese technique, *furoshiki*. It's reusable, creates no waste and it's far more pleasant spending an afternoon folding and tying than dealing with scissors, paper and tape. I use pieces of cotton and linen fabric as the cloth is strong enough to support a little weight and, as it's opaque, no one can see what's inside the parcel. Pieces of fabric cut from old clothing or bed linen also work well, or seek out vintage fabrics, dish towels and silk scarves for something a little bit different. You can find how-to *furoshiki* videos on YouTube, which are particularly useful for wrapping unusual shapes or bottles. I like to add a couple of natural touches to the knot – a stem of eucalyptus, a tiny pine cone, a slice of dried orange (see page 66 for the how-to) or a handmade gift tag.

_____

<u>Other ideas for sustainable gift wrapping</u>

* Keep hold of any gift bags or boxes you have previously received and reuse. Why not ask friends, family members or work colleagues if they would like to do a gift bag swap?

* Make a cracker (see page 54) for small treats like secret Santa.

* For kids, repurpose old comics or posters.

* Pages from old newspapers and magazines.

* Old delivery packaging (that's still in good reusable condition) can be given a new lease of life with some Christmas stamps and eco-friendly inks. Finish with some ribbon.

* Family members would be delighted to receive a present wrapped in a child's artwork from nursery, or ask your kids to get crafty and design their own wrapping paper.

* If you can sew, repurpose old tablecloths or duvet covers into reusable fabric gift bags can be used again and again.

* If you need to buy new paper for wrapping, choose rolls of recyclable brown kraft paper or tissue paper that can be composted afterwards.

* Fasten parcels with twine made from jute or hemp, leftover pieces of yarn or biodegradable washi tape.

Gifting Ideas

No matter the occasion, I try my best to give presents that are ethical and sustainable. Here are some ideas for greener gift giving:

————————

Donate: Buy a membership to an animal welfare or environmental charity. Make a donation to local charitable initiatives – conservation projects, community gardens or a nature reserve.

Choose experiences over material goods: Gift cinema or theatre tickets, or a restaurant voucher for a family meal. Book an escape-room experience or a trampoline park. Buy a membership to an art gallery, theatre, cinema or museum. Book an in-person workshop to learn a new skill, such as pottery, breadmaking, or photography. Alternatively, gift an online class – there are thousands available, from famous authors teaching writing and filmmakers on making movies, to sewing classes and painting watercolours.

Future gifts: Offer your services to a family member or a friend. It could be for an evening babysitting or a day pet sitting. Ask them if they need help around the house or in the garden. Make them a meal, or go out for a picnic lunch. Take the kids for day out or invite your friends to a tea party. Get family or friends together and arrange to do something memorable later in the year. Divide the cost between you to keep it budget friendly.

Subscription gifts: If you are buying for someone with a specific interest but don't know what to get them, look to small businesses that offer subscription gifts. You can find everything from books, breadmaking and cocktails to flowers and chocolates.

Secondhand gifts: Prioritize shopping for secondhand gifts. It's budget friendly and sustainable. Vintage pieces show the recipient that you've bought with intention. Look for refurbished items: musical instruments, technology, camera equipment and bikes that have been safely restored.

* For adults: Search third-party seller apps and websites, charity shops and thrift stores for vintage vinyl, classic video games, books, sports equipment, clothing and homewares. If you are unsure what someone may like, opt for a gift card from a vintage store or charity shop.

* For kids: Scour local buy-nothing pages, charity shops and thrift stores for toys and furniture that can be upcycled. Dolls houses, blackboards, wooden toy kitchens and garages, small tables or desks can all be given a new lease of life using paint and wallpaper offcuts or samples. Vintage stores are great places to find board games and car boots are good for character toys and building blocks, while third-party selling apps offer an enormous selection of character clothing, homeware and toys.

Give less: One of the simplest ways to be greener is to not buy lots of extras. If your child has asked for one specific toy, that's what they are really looking for, not lots of cheap plastic items that will be relegated to the bottom of the toybox (toychest). A useful mantra to consider when buying for kids is 'something they want, something they need, something to wear, something to read'. If the children in your family are not big book readers, look at magazines and comic subscriptions, or colouring and puzzle books.

Simple stocking filler: Make your own play dough using ingredients you may already have in the cupboard. To make one ball, add 250g (9oz) plain flour (all-purpose flour), 250ml (8.5fl oz) water, 2 tsp cream of tartar, 150g (5¼oz) table salt, 1 tbsp vegetable oil and a few drops of food colouring to a medium-sized saucepan. On a medium heat, stir consistently with a wooden spoon until the ingredients start to thicken and come together into a ball. Turn off the heat. Place the ball on a lightly floured surface and knead until smooth. Once cool, store in an airtight container at room temperature.

Shopping for teens: Look for accessories made from upcycled or natural fabrics, headbands, gloves and bags are good options. Technology fans might like to get their hands on a sustainably made turntable, headphones or speakers. Teens love comfortable clothing, so choose simply designed t-shirts or hoodies from ethical fashion brands. Opt for practical gifts, such as compostable phone covers, a recycled laptop case or sustainable sunglasses. Head to your local zero waste store for reusable make-up pads, eco-friendly make up and organic skincare products. If your teen likes skateboarding or snowboarding, look for boards made from sustainable bamboo.

Low-waste gifts: Head to zero-waste stores to find handmade soaps, eco-friendly candles, refillable natural beauty products and edible gifts. These are also great places to source sustainable coffee cups, string shopping bags and shaving accessories.

Grow: Put together packets of seeds based on an interest or hobby and tie them together with jute twine. Add a simple sprig of dried lavender or rosemary for decoration. For herbal tea fans, choose packets of chamomile, fennel, lemon balm and peppermint seeds. For an extra touch, arrange the herb packets in a vintage teacup. If you are buying for a cook, choose a Mediterranean combination of flavours such as basil, marjoram and oregano or Indian herbs such as coriander, curry leaves and fenugreek. Add a nice bottle of olive oil or rapeseed (canola) oil to complete the gift. For flower lovers, a bouquet of preserved blooms makes a great alternative to buying fresh flowers, which have a large carbon footprint.

Edibles: Put together hampers of local products such as cheeses, crackers, preserves, chutney and honey. Collect thrifted baskets to fill with homemade produce. Old jam (jelly) jars, pickle jars, and oil bottles with stoppers can be sterilized and refilled with homemade pickles, flavoured oils, vinegars and jams. Send beer lovers a crate of craft beer brewed from leftover bread or gift a subscription to a natural wine club.

Make your own beauty products: Rather than buying commercial gift packs of body lotion and bubble bath, have a go at making your own. Look online for tutorials to create your own bath oils or lotions. Gather flowers and herbs throughout the summer to give them time to dry out. Rose petals, lavender stems, calendula, chamomile and eucalyptus all work well for this.

Regifting: This works particularly well with unwanted kids' presents, accessories and beauty gift sets. If it's a duplicate or is not going to be used and is still in good condition, regift it (although be mindful not to give it back to the person who gifted it to you originally!).

Lavender & Lemon Sea Salt Scrub

This scrub makes the perfect low-waste gift for Christmas and is ideal as a thank-you present for teachers. Use a recycled jam (jelly) jar, fill with the scrub, add a small sprig of dried lavender on top for a pretty touch, seal and decorate with a gift tag listing the ingredients.

————

Makes one jar
You will need
125g (½ cup) coarse sea salt
5½ tbsp sweet almond oil
1 bowl and a spoon
5–10 drops lavender essential oil*
5–10 drops lemon essential oil
Zest of 1 unwaxed lemon
A few dried lavender flowers
1 clean jar with a lid

HOW TO

1. Mix the sea salt with the almond oil in a bowl.

2. Add the essential oils and mix again. Stir through the lemon zest and the dried lavender flowers.

3. Transfer to a clean jar and seal.

Note
You may also want to include an instructions label:

To use
Pop a little of the scrub on your fingertips and gently rub on to wet skin in a circular motion to remove any dead cells. Rinse off and gently pat dry with a towel.

Use within one month of making.

*See note on pets and essential oils, page 29.

Lavender, Peppermint & Rosemary Soap Bar

Soap-making is quick and easy using the 'melt and pour' method. It doesn't require any specialized equipment and is a great way to get creative. I use an entire 1kg (2lb 4oz) bar because that fits my mould but you can reduce the quantities in the recipe for the size of mould you intend to use.

————————

There are lots of different melt-and-pour soap bars available, but not all of them are good for the environment. Many contain palm oil or mineral oil (a by-product of petroleum) and others are derived from GMO crops or contain animal fats. I like to use a base that is vegan, non-GMO and free from palm oil and synthetic surfactants. My soap base of choice is made with argan oil as it is rich in vitamin E and very nourishing for skin.

Any item that holds water can be repurposed as a mould for soap making – muffin tins (pans), yoghurt pots, vintage jelly (jello) moulds or patisserie tins, and plastic sandwich boxes all work well. I use a silicone loaf pan that can hold 1.2 kg (2lb 10oz) of soap, and this makes 12 bars.

I like to add a sprinkling of dried lavender flowers, poppy seeds and herbs to the mix as it looks pretty, but these are not essential.

Makes 12 bars

You will need

1kg (2lb 4oz) bar melt-and-pour soap

Knife

Large heavy-based saucepan

Spoon

20 drops lavender essential oil*

20 drops peppermint essential oil

20 drops rosemary essential oil

Pinch of finely chopped dried lavender flowers, peppermint, rosemary leaves and poppy seeds (optional)

Soap mould

HOW TO

1. Cut the melt-and-pour soap into chunks and add to the saucepan. Gently heat the saucepan and start to melt the soap. Once the soap has fully melted you need to work quickly and add the essential oils and the botanical elements.

2. Add the essential oils (and the dried flowers, poppy seeds, and herbs if using). Stir quickly to avoid a skin forming on the surface of the soap.

3. Pour carefully and slowly into the prepared soap mould. Set aside and leave to cool at room temperature for 48 hours.

4. Remove from the mould – or cut into bars if using a silicone loaf pan – and wrap in greaseproof paper.

*See note on pets and essential oils, page 29.

Vegan Peppermint Lip Balm

I used to carry a small container of petroleum jelly with me everywhere. I never once considered that it was a by-product of the crude-oil extraction process (obviously the clue is in the name!). Yet, once I understood how the product was made, I had to stop buying it.

———————

Natural lip balms are traditionally made with beeswax or plant-based wax. These waxes are added to stabilize and emulsify balms and lotions, and they also make lip balms shine. For this recipe, I've used candelilla wax, which is derived from the leaves of the candelilla shrub. It is completely natural and suitable for vegans, and as it is harder than beeswax, you only need to use a little to achieve similar results.

In addition to the candelilla wax, I have used sweet almond oil, which softens lips, and shea butter to moisturize and heal. If you want, you can add a few drops of essential oil for a scented balm, but avoid using spicy oils such as clove or ginger as these can cause a burning sensation. Citrus oils should also be avoided as they are phototoxic and can make skin more sensitive to the sun. I use peppermint for my lip balm as it is warming for cold winter lips.

Makes three tins/jars

You will need

3 tbsp sweet almond oil

1 tbsp unrefined organic shea butter

½ tbsp candelilla wax

Heatproof jar (I use an old jam (jelly) jar)

Saucepan

Spoon

5 drops peppermint essential oil*

Lip-balm tins or small wide-mouth glass jars

HOW TO

1. Place the sweet almond oil, shea butter and candelilla wax into the heatproof jar. Set the jar down into a saucepan filled with around 5cm (2in) of water to create a makeshift double boiler. Gently heat the pan and once the ingredients start to melt, stir with the spoon.

2. Remove the jar from the pan. Wipe away any water from the outside of the jar to prevent drips when pouring the mixture into the tins.

3. Add the peppermint essential oil, then stir again with the spoon to combine.

4. Pour the mixture into the lip-balm tins or wide-mouth glass jars and leave to cool.

5. The lip balm should solidify in around an hour. Once it is completely solid, it is ready to use.

Notes

You can buy new tins or glass jars for this lip-balm recipe, or reuse ones you already have. If you are reusing containers, remove any waxy debris and then sterilize in boiling water for three to four minutes before filling with the new mixture.

The shelf life of this lip balm is around six months. But always check the use-by date of the ingredients you are using as this may be shorter.

*See note on pets and essential oils, page 29.

No-Sew Herbal Sleep Sachet

Lavender and chamomile are two of my favourite plants to grow in the garden. They are beautiful and highly productive, provide vital nectar for pollinating insects, and have a wonderful aroma. Both lavender and chamomile can be harvested and dried, then used as a remedy to reduce stress and prevent sleeplessness. Towards the end of the growing season, I like to pick a few flower buds and use them to make these herbal sleep sachets.

———

I've used some leftover linen fabric for this crafting project, but you can use any natural fabric you have to hand. If you don't grow either plant in the garden, you can find dried organic lavender and chamomile buds in health-food stores or online.

Makes four pillows
You will need
1 large bunch dried lavender
1 large bunch dried chamomile flowers
Mixing bowl
Spoon
Fusible hem tape
8 squares of fabric, 10 x 10cm (4 x 4in)
Tea towel (lightly dampened)
Iron and ironing board
Pinking shears

HOW TO

1. Strip the flower buds from the dried lavender and chamomile and add to the mixing bowl.

2. Cut 16 strips of fusible hem tape to fit each side of your fabric squares.

3. Place one of the fabric squares, right side down on top of the ironing board (so the wrong side of the fabric faces up).

4. Place a strip of hem tape on three of the four sides of the square and up against the edges of the fabric.

5. Put another piece of fabric right side facing up, on top of the first piece of fabric, lining up the edges.

6. Pop the dampened tea towel over the top of the fabric square and iron to seal the three sides.

7. Fill the sachet with 1–2 tbsp of dried lavender and chamomile mix.

8. To close the sachet, place the remaining piece of fusible hem tape into the opening. Lay the damp tea towel over this area only, and iron to seal. Be careful not to iron the dried materials.

9. Cut around the edges with pinking shears for a neater finish.

To use
Simply place one of these lavender and chamomile sachets inside a pillowcase to aid a better night's sleep. Gently squeeze the pillow to release the fragrance.

These sachets are also useful placed in a closet, laundry basket or chest of drawers to help repel moths. Keep out of the reach of babies, children and pets.

Wildflower Container

In the UK wildflowers are being lost at a rapid rate and one in five are under threat. Only 3% of flower meadows that existed in the 1930s remain*. The picture is similar worldwide and when wildflowers perish, vital food sources and habitats are destroyed.

———————

Gifting wildflower seeds is an easy way to help bring these much-needed plants back to our gardens. You can also make your own seed bombs (see page 96 for the how-to). Look for nurseries specializing in native wildflowers and check that the seeds have local provenance.

Wildflower seeds can be scattered to create meadows and replace lawns, and can also be used in raised beds and containers. Every summer I plant patio pots and window boxes with wildflowers, and when they are filled with beautiful blooms, I like to observe the bees and other pollinating insects feasting on the nectar.

If you are planning to make a wildflower container for a gift, choose the largest one you can find as wildflowers need space to grow. I like to scour vintage and salvage fairs for old tin baths and wooden crates that can be repurposed for this gardening project. Make sure to include a label explaining how to look after your container.

You will need

Large container with drainage holes
Stones/broken crockery or terracotta pots
Potting compost
Native wildflower seeds

HOW TO

1. Line the bottom of your container with a few pieces of broken terracotta pot or stones.

2. Fill the container with potting compost and sprinkle the wildflower seeds over the surface of the compost.

3. Lightly cover the seeds with a little more potting compost and water well.

How to look after your container

Water your wildflower seeds twice a week, keeping the potting compost damp while the seeds germinate. You may need to water more frequently in warm weather.

*The Wildflower Garden, part of Plantlife, a charity working to save threatened plants: www.plantlife.org.uk.

Upcycled Terrarium

A terrarium is a wonderful way to welcome nature indoors. You can purchase ready-made glass terrariums, but it's easy to upcycle an old jam (jelly) jar, coffee jar or glass vase and make your own. Small-sized terrariums filled with succulents make wonderful gifts for friends or teachers – just remember to attach a label with care instructions.

―――――――

Many plant varieties grow happily in a terrarium. Look for plants that enjoy drier conditions, such as cacti, air plants and succulents. Search online for specialist nurseries that grow baby plants for terrariums.

I use a layer of alpine grit for drainage purposes, but pebbles and gravel also work well. If you are growing cacti or succulents, it's worth investing in a specialist potting compost. For other plants, use a good-quality indoor peat-free potting mix.

You will need

Glass vessel

Alpine grit

Indoor potting mix or cactus compost

Large spoon

Selection of small plants – e.g. *Echeveria* 'Blue Sky', zebra cactus (*Haworthia*), donkey's tail (*Sedum morganianum* 'Burrito')

Teaspoon

HOW TO

1. Wash your chosen container in warm, soapy water. Rinse, then set aside to air dry.

2. Place a thin layer of alpine grit in the bottom of the container.

3. Next, add a layer of indoor potting mix or cactus compost approximately three times the depth of the layer of the alpine grit.

4. Using the large spoon, hollow out a hole in the potting mix for each plant. Place plants in the holes and pat the soil firmly around the roots of each plant.

5. Cover the compost with a second layer of alpine grit.

6. Water each plant with a teaspoon of water.

How to care for your terrarium

Keep out of direct sunlight. Check the soil moisture level every two weeks. If the soil is completely dry, water each plant with a teaspoon of water.

Houseplants

Houseplants are the superheroes in our homes. They have the power to reduce levels of indoor air pollution and to help lower stress, as well as making a home feel calmer and more relaxed. Houseplants also last longer than a bunch of flowers or a box of chocolates, and gifting one to someone we care for is a symbol of friendship and trust.

————————

These are a few of my favourite houseplants that are easy to look after and have excellent air purifying properties:

Spider plant (*Chlorophytum comosum 'Variegatum'*) Tolerant of both light and shade. Avoid direct sunlight, which can scorch the leaves. Feed monthly with organic liquid fertilizer in spring and summer but dilute by half the recommended amount as it prefers a weaker feed. Spider plants develop baby plantlets regularly; simply pinch these off and replant them in compost to create new plants.

Peace lily (*Spathiphyllum*) Likes indirect sunlight and shade. Especially good in bathrooms, where it thrives in humid conditions, but equally happy elsewhere if it gets a regular misting with water. Take care not to overwater.

Sweetheart plant (*Philodendron scandens*) Likes indirect sunlight and to be watered as soon as the top of the soil is dry to the touch. In spring and summer, feed monthly with an organic liquid fertilizer. Can be trained to climb upwards or left to trail.

Snake plant/Mother-in-law's tongue (*Sansavieria trifasciata*) Slow-growing and one of the best plants for improving indoor air pollution. Prefers bright light but can handle some shade, too. Snake plants like to have their roots crowded, so choose a tight-fitting container. Use good-quality cactus compost and feed once a month from spring to autumn (fall). Water sparingly in autumn and winter.

Wildflower Seed Bombs

Wildflower seed bombs are easy to make and a useful way to reuse old newspapers or junk mail. When these bombs are planted in soil or a container, you can create a little patch of wildflower heaven for pollinating insects.

———————

This project can get a little messy, so wear an apron. You can use any recyclable paper, including school worksheets, grocery store bags or tissue paper. I've rolled these seed bombs into balls but if you are giving them as a Christmas present, you can use a cookie cutter or silicone mould to form specific shapes.

You will need
Recyclable paper
Scissors
Large bowl
Water
Electric blender/food processor
Strainer
Cloth
Native wildflower seeds
Cookie cutters/silicone mould (optional)
Reusable sponge (optional)
Dish towel or cooling rack

HOW TO

1. Cut your paper into small pieces and place in a bowl.

2. Add water to the bowl, ensuring that the paper is saturated.

3. Leave the paper to soak for 30 minutes.

4. Tip the soaked paper into the blender or food processor. Add more water to cover the paper, then blend to a pulp.

5. Place the strainer over the bowl. Pop a cloth on the bottom of the strainer. Remove the pulp from the blender or food processor and place it on the cloth.

6. Add 2–3 tbsp of native wildflower seeds to the pulp. Fold the cloth is half and squeeze out any excess water. The mixture should be moist but not soaking wet.

7. Roll the pulp into small-sized balls or push into cookie cutters or silicone moulds. If you choose to use a cutter or mould, you may need to remove excess water. To do this, press down firmly on each bomb with a sponge. Gently remove the cookie cutter to reuse it.

8. Place each seed bomb on a dish towel or cooling rack to dry. This should take approximately two days.

How to plant

9. Plant outdoors in spring in a flower bed or container, or indoors in a container placed on a sunny windowsill.

10. Dig a hole roughly the size of your seed bomb. Place the bomb in the hole and cover with compost. Water well.

11. Keep the soil moist for the first few weeks after planting.

12. You should see signs of germination in two to three weeks.

Note
Add a label with planting instructions if you are gifting the seed bombs.

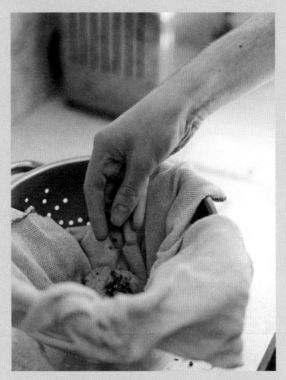

CONSIDERED GIFTING

Eat,
Drink &
Be Merry

WE HAVE A QUIET, CALM AND
RELAXING MEAL WHICH WE LOOK
FORWARD TO EVERY YEAR

Eat, Drink & Be Merry

Our celebrations are kept intentionally small, with only three of us around the dinner table. We cook a vegetarian main course served with roast potatoes, parsnips and Brussels sprouts, usually followed by a crumble topped mince pie and a big dollop of cream. I set the table with some greenery and candles (see page 50) and we have a quiet, calm and relaxing meal which we look forward to every year. It wasn't always this way, and we spent many torturous festive seasons dealing with difficult relatives and eating lackluster meals. Feasting at Christmas is a treat and should bring you joy. If it doesn't, then maybe it's time to make some changes.

Every year lots of people gather around the dining table for a traditional Christmas dinner. Yet, many dread the day and are reluctant to admit that they would rather do something else. Have a conversation with your family or guests and find out if they would prefer a different meal or perhaps go to a restaurant.

Often the responsibility falls on one person to cook Christmas dinner, and they are trapped in the kitchen over the holidays, missing out on all the fun and not enjoying the experience at all. This makes them understandably resentful, and many dread the festive season for this reason. If this is you, it's time to tell others how you feel. There is no rulebook for Christmas food, and it simply doesn't matter if everyone sits down together and eats the same meal. Why not keep Christmas Day free to enjoy the festivities and have meals that can easily be put together instead? Make a large pot of curry, a pizza or a pasta dish.

If you are cooking on Christmas Day, it's useful to do some preparation in advance. Vegetables and main courses can be made the day before, allowing you to simply reheat when required. To help with the preparation or to keep costs down, ask everyone who is coming to dinner to contribute a dish or a component of the meal.

When you are out shopping for festive food, visit your greengrocer or farmer's market for seasonal produce. Buying fresh food from a local grower or farmer helps to reduce your carbon footprint substantially as there is no need for any transportation, food miles or refrigeration.

The difference in the taste of fresh produce is incredible and nutrient levels are significantly higher than those that have been stored for some time. Support your local refill store where you can use your own packaging and shop for nuts, dried fruit, spices, cereals and baking products. When we stop giving our money to these wonderful local businesses, we end up potentially losing another hardworking shopkeeper or producer and our towns and cities struggle more.

The best way to someone's heart is through their stomach, so why not give someone you care about an edible gift? These gifts are thoughtful, creative and personal, and could be anything from a homemade loaf of bread and a jar of jam to a box of handmade crackers alongside a piece of local cheese.

In this chapter you'll find lots of ideas for making your own gifts, including the recipes for two of my favourites – salted caramel fudge and pear and ginger chutney. Spending time creating in the kitchen and listening to Christmas music is a lovely ritual that allows you to slow down and celebrate the festive season in a more considered way.

———————

Christmas Food & Reducing Waste

The holidays can last for a long time, and you may have a lot of people to feed, so get ahead with meal planning. Create a list of ingredients to take with you to the supermarket or grocery store. Only buy and cook what you need. This helps keep things budget friendly too. If you have groceries delivered, make sure to book a delivery slot early.

———————

* <u>Clear out your fridge and freezer</u>: Get rid of old jars that linger in the back of the fridge and make scratch-it meals from leftovers. Give the fridge a good clean with the winter multi-purpose cleaning spray on page 28.

* <u>Batch cook</u>: In the run-up to the holidays; soups, stews, pasta sauces and curries are all good. Make enough for two meals and stick one in the freezer for later. This makes more economical use of heating the oven, too. Future you will be grateful for meals that are ready to go when you are exhausted and can't face cooking.

Christmas generates an enormous amount of food waste, and we should all aim to reduce what we throw away.

<u>Here are some useful ideas to help with this</u>:

* <u>Plan</u>: Work out how many people are coming to Christmas dinner. Young children will likely eat less than adults, so consider portion sizes, too.

* <u>Skip a dish or two</u>: If no one likes a particular dish but it's traditional to serve them, don't! They won't be missed.

* <u>Donate</u>: Give away any unopened leftover foodstuffs to food banks or offer it up for free on third party apps.

* <u>Get savvy</u>: Buy frozen produce or tinned foods rather than fresh. These are cheaper, longer lasting and taste pretty good also.

* <u>Potatoes</u>: Parboil potatoes and arrange them on a baking sheet. Pop in the freezer until solid, then transfer to a freezer bag. They can be cooked from frozen. Use within a month. Leftover mashed potato can also be frozen and will keep for a month (defrost before heating).

* <u>Brussels sprouts</u>: To freeze sprouts, peel, then blanch in boiling water for 2–4 minutes. Plunge into a bowl of cold water, drain and then freeze. Peel and chop sprouts in half and add to stir fries, or roast for 30 minutes in the oven and mix through risottos. They are also delicious shredded and added to bubble and squeak cakes.

* <u>Leave no waste</u>: Roasted vegetables – turn into a mixed vegetable soup. Leftover roasted potatoes, carrots, swede, parsnips and greens can all be cooked in vegetable stock and then blended to a creamy consistency. Perfect for taking in a flask for a boxing day walk. Alternatively, add the roasted vegetables to pasta, couscous or bulghar wheat along with some chopped herbs, grated cheese and a little salad dressing for lunch boxes.

* <u>Keep the peel</u>: Carrots, parsnips, beetroot (beets), potatoes and sweet potato peel are all perfect for making your own crisps. Mix in a bowl with a little olive oil and salt, then place on a baking sheet and bake in the oven at 200°C/400°F/gas mark 6 for eight to 10 minutes.

* <u>Bread</u>: Use any leftover slices or crusts to make breadcrumbs. Stick them in the food processor and roughly chop. Use breadcrumbs for making burgers and meatballs. Alternatively, mix chunkier size breadcrumbs through a little olive oil and place them on a baking tray. Roast in a medium oven for around 20 minutes or until golden. Serve on top of pasta dishes or casseroles for extra crunch.

* <u>Christmas cake or pudding</u>: Crumble into ice cream or porridge. Add small cubes to brownie or muffin recipes. Leftover Christmas pudding can be frozen in individual slices for up to 3 months. Defrost slices in the fridge overnight before reheating. You can also use Christmas pudding as a crumble topping.

* <u>Cheese</u>: Gather cheese offcuts and large crumbs and pop them in a freezer bag. Store in the freezer and add to the bag whenever you have leftovers. These make a great sauce for macaroni or cauliflower cheese and work well on top of pizzas. Add the rind from parmesan to soups and stews to give extra flavour. Turn leftover Cheddar cheese into scones or make it into savoury cheese and chive dumplings to top casseroles and stews.

* <u>Feed the birds</u>: Give the birds a treat by feeding them with Christmas leftovers. They will happily feast on cold roast potatoes chopped into small pieces as well as sweet treats like mince pies, fruit cakes and Christmas pudding.

Reusable Bowl Covers

Clingfilm (plastic wrap) is one of those useful kitchen items that many of us use to cover leftovers. Unfortunately, it can't be recycled due to the combination of chemicals and resins in the plastic, which can't be separated, and ends up in landfill where it takes hundreds of years to degrade.

––––––––

If you don't have any spare containers for leftovers or want to save on washing up, use a dinner plate or side plate to cover the top of a bowl before putting it in the fridge. If you prefer a more secure option, you can buy or make reusable bowl covers.

These are simply covers made from cotton that pop over the top of the bowl, with an elastic cord to hold them in place. They come in a range of sizes and are machine washable so can be used repeatedly.

I like to make my own from old dish towels that have developed holes, as I can utilize the surrounding fabric. Old cotton shirts, tablecloths and bedding are also good options for making your own. Any leftover scraps of fabric can be used as cleaning rags or added to the compost bin.

There are no specific measurements for these covers, but you will need a piece of fabric that will fit across the width of your chosen bowl plus an additional 5cm (2in) to fasten over the sides of the bowl. I use organic cotton thread and elastic to make these covers, but you can use whatever thread or elastic you already own.

continues overleaf...

You will need

Iron
Fabric scraps
Bowl
Ruler
Fabric marker pen/chalk
Fabric scissors
Pins
Sewing machine
Organic cotton elastic
Safety pin
Needle
Organic cotton thread
Pins

HOW TO

1. Iron your chosen fabric to ensure a flat surface.

2. Lay the bowl upside down on the wrong side of the fabric (the side of the fabric that will not be visible).

3. Using the ruler, measure 5cm (2in) from the outside of the bowl and mark the spot with your fabric marker pen/chalk.

4. Do this at regular intervals around the bowl, then connect the dots to form a circle around the bowl.

5. Cut around this line with fabric scissors, until you have a circle of fabric.

6. Fold the edges of your fabric inwards approximately 2cm (¾in) and pin in place. You will need to do this all the way round the fabric, leaving a 5cm (2in) opening at the end.

7. Using the sewing machine, sew a simple stitch around the edge of the folded fabric.

8. Measure the elastic around the outside of the bowl and subtract 5cm (2in) from the figure. Cut the elastic to the reduced length.

9. Hook a safety pin to one end of the elastic and then insert this into the opening of the bowl cover.

10. Guide the safety pin around the seam until the pin and the elastic come through the other side.

11. Stitch the two ends of the elastic together using a needle and thread.

12. Fold the opening in the fabric over the elastic and sew to close.

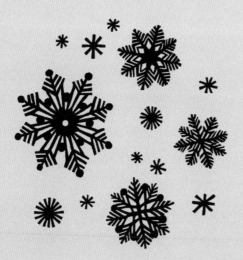

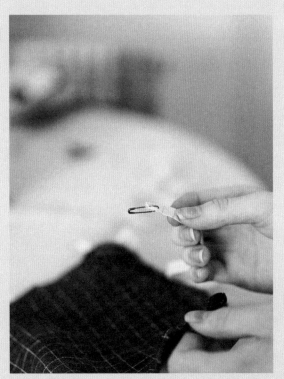

EAT, DRINK & BE MERRY

Edible Gifts

Buying edible gifts can be expensive, but you can easily make things at home that will help lower the cost significantly. From foraging for wild berries and buying in bulk, to utilizing past-its-best produce and homegrown vegetables, you can make delicious treats and reduce food waste at the same time.

———

I've listed a few ideas below to get you started, and you can find lots of recipes for these online.

Learning to preserve is a wonderful skill to possess, and once you get the hang of it, you can turn produce into something delectable. Keep hold of jars throughout the year that you can re-use for gifting (see page 118 for how to sterilize them).

* In autumn (fall), gather rosehips to make into a syrup, crab apples, sloes and damsons to turn into hedgerow jelly, or blackberries to make jam or add to vodka and gins.

* In summer, berries and stone fruits are at their peak and less expensive. Buy in bulk or visit a pick-your-own farm and use the fruit to make jams and syrups.

* Add unripe pears to some cider along with cloves and cinnamon to make jars of mulled pears.

* Dry tomatoes slowly in the oven and add to a jar of olive oil and marjoram.

* Turn citrus fruits into marmalade and curds or make jars of preserved lemons.

* Make sauerkraut or kimchi from cabbage leaves.

* Turn shrivelled mushrooms or tomatoes into homemade ketchup and sauces.

* Pickle shallots or small onions.

* Turn autumnal squashes, pumpkins and carrots into chutney or relish.

* Use past-their-best produce or vegetable gluts.

From the storecupboard:

* Make jars of salted caramel or chocolate sauce.

* Bake crackers and flavour them with homegrown herbs. Gift alongside a nice piece of cheese.

* Roast chickpeas with a mixture of spices for a quick and healthy snack option.

* Put together brownie or cookie mixes. Combine layers of the ingredients needed for the bake in larger glass jars along with cooking instructions.

* Bake shortbread or biscuits and add some seasonal spices for a festive kick.

* Gift a sourdough starter to those who like breadmaking. You can find these online from independent bakeries.

* Don't forget to include a label with the ingredients and instructions for storage for each edible gift you make.

Christmas Cake

Making a Christmas cake is a slow, mindful experience. It requires both time and patience as you need to pay attention to each stage of the recipe for it to turn out well. It's worth the effort though, as you will be rewarded with a delicious and moist cake, and everyone who has a slice will want another one.

———————

The dried fruit in the cake needs to be marinated overnight in alcohol to soak up all the flavours. You can use brandy, sherry, rum, whisky or orange liqueur, whichever you prefer. If you plan to add a layer of marzipan and icing to the cake later, I recommend using lemon curd rather than jam (jelly) to sandwich the layers together.

Makes one 23cm (9in) Christmas cake
Ingredients
220g (7¾oz) raisins
250g (9oz) currants
250g (9oz) sultanas
200ml (7fl oz) alcohol (brandy, sherry, rum, whisky, orange liqueur…)
100g (3½oz) glacé cherries, chopped
60g (2¼oz) flaked almonds, chopped
220g (7¾oz) plain flour
115g (4oz) unsalted butter, softened
175g (6oz) soft light brown sugar
1 lemon, zested
1 orange, zested
1 tbsp treacle
4 medium free-range eggs
½ tsp mixed spice
½ tsp ground nutmeg
½ tsp salt

continues overleaf…

HOW TO

1. Add the raisins, currants and sultanas to a large bowl. Pour over your alcohol of choice. Cover the bowl with a large plate and leave overnight.

2. The next day, grease and line a 23cm (9in) cake tin (pan). Cut two further pieces of baking paper that are the size of the bottom of the tin. Set these two pieces of baking paper aside for later.

3. Preheat the oven to 140°C (275°F)/120°C (250°F) fan/gas mark 1.

4. Add the glacé cherries and flaked almonds to the bowl with the dried fruit.

5. Add 1 tbsp of flour and mix, then set aside.

6. In a separate mixing bowl, cream together the butter and the sugar. Add lemon zest, orange zest and treacle. Mix to combine.

7. Lightly beat the eggs in a separate bowl. Add a little of the eggs along with 1 tbsp of flour to the mixing bowl containing the butter and sugar and beat well with a wooden spoon. Repeat this method until all the egg has been added.

8. Sieve the rest of the flour, mixed spice, nutmeg and salt into the mixing bowl.

9. Fold the flour mix in with a metal spoon.

10. Add the bowl of dried fruit to the mixing bowl. Mix well.

11. Tip the mixture into the prepared cake tin and smooth the surface.

12. Using a wooden spoon, make a gentle hollow in the middle of the mixture (this helps the top of the cake stay flat for decorating).

13. Place the two round pieces of baking paper on top of the cake mix.

14. Cook for around three-and-a-half hours or until a cake skewer comes out clean.

15. Leave to cool for one hour in the tin. Remove and place on a wire rack.

Lemon & Thyme Infused Oil

Whenever I need to perk up some homegrown or leftover salad leaves this oil is my go-to. It is delicious drizzled over pasta dishes and risottos or added to any cream-based sauce. It's also a great recipe for using up any lemons after you have juiced them as it is the peel that flavours the oil.

———————

Makes one 250ml (9fl oz) bottle

Ingredients

2 unwaxed lemons

250ml (9fl oz) rapeseed (canola) oil

4–6 sprigs of fresh thyme or lemon thyme

Lemon extract (optional)

HOW TO

1. Wash the lemons and peel the skins. Put the peel and the oil into a small saucepan. Gently heat for 10 minutes, but do not allow it to boil.

2. Take off the heat, add the thyme sprigs and allow to cool completely.

3. Taste the oil for flavour, if it is a little bitter or you prefer a stronger lemon flavour, add a few drops of lemon extract. You can find lemon extract in the baking section of the supermarket.

4. When cool, remove the thyme sprigs and the lemon peel. Transfer the flavoured oil to a sterilized glass jar or bottle (see page 118) and seal with a lid. Keeps for one month.

Clementine & Rosemary Infused Gin

I use festive clementines for this gin recipe, but you can swap them out for lemons, limes, grapefruit, tangerines or oranges if you prefer. Use a peeler if you have one, as this helps to remove the pith cleanly from the citrus. The pith has a bitter flavour that can affect the final taste of the infusion. If you are peeling by hand, try to pick off any excess pith before adding the peel to the gin.

———————

Use a good-quality bottle of gin from the supermarket but avoid anything that contains lots of extra botanical ingredients as this won't allow the citrus and rosemary to infuse properly.

You can reuse any small miniature bottles you have for this recipe. Remove old labels and wash the bottles thoroughly with warm, soapy water. Rinse well and leave them to air dry. You will also need a muslin cloth for straining the gin before bottling. You can find new bottles and muslin cloths online or from craft stores. If you already have a muslin cloth, make sure that it is clean and has been sterilized by boiling in water for five minutes before use.

To fully appreciate the depth of flavour, drink the gin neat, but it's also delicious added to tonic or lemonade for something light and refreshing.

Ingredients
2 clementines (or other citrus fruit)
2 sprigs of rosemary
170cl bottle gin

HOW TO

1. Peel the clementines. Remove any pith from the peel. Set aside the fruit to eat later. If you are using lemons or limes, squeeze the juice and pop in the fridge or freezer.

2. Place the citrus peel in a large glass jar (or a jug or bottle). Add the rosemary sprigs.

3. Pour the bottle of gin over the citrus and rosemary.

4. Pop the lid on the jar.

5. Keep the jar somewhere dark for two to three weeks.

6. After two weeks, have a taste to determine the strength of the flavour. If you prefer a stronger rosemary taste, leave the gin to infuse for a further week.

7. Once you are happy with the balance of flavours, it's time to bottle it up. Place a piece of muslin cloth into a sieve. Sit the sieve over the top of a jug, then pour the infusion through.

8. Pour the jug of infused gin into the miniature bottles and seal.

9. To decorate, tie a little twine around each bottle neck and attach a label with the list of ingredients.

Pear & Ginger Chutney

Making chutney is a great way to use up any gluts or leftover pieces of fruit and veg. We always seem to have pears lurking in the fruit bowl, and as they never seem to ripen, we use them for baking or in this chutney recipe. Pear and ginger is a warm and spicy partnership, ideal for bringing comfort on a cold winter's day.

————————

Feel free to swap out the pears for the same quantity of apples, rhubarb or tomatoes if you prefer. I'm a sultana fan, so I like to add those to the mixture, but you could also use raisins or mixed dried fruit instead. If you like a hot chutney, throw in some chilli flakes when adding the ginger to the pan.

This chutney is a delicious accompaniment to cheeses, added to sandwiches or served on the side with curry and naan bread. It is simple to make and is a perfect addition to a homemade hamper.

Makes four small jars*

Ingredients

225g (8oz) dark brown soft sugar

225ml (8¾fl oz) apple cider vinegar

1 tsp mixed spice

30g (1oz) ginger, peeled and chopped finely

1 tsp ground ginger

3 shallots, finely diced

75g (2½oz) sultanas

5 pears, cored and chopped into small cubes

HOW TO

1. Add the sugar, apple cider vinegar and mixed spice to a medium-sized saucepan.

2. Heat the mixture, stirring occasionally until it comes to a simmer.

3. Add the chopped ginger, ground ginger and the shallots to the pan, stir to combine.

4. Simmer gently for approximately 10 minutes until the liquid has reduced by half.

5. Add the dried fruit and the chopped pears and stir to combine.

6. Simmer once again until the pears are soft, and you have reached the desired consistency.

7. Decant the chutney into hot sterilized jars and seal.

8. Store in a cool, dark place. Once opened, keep in the fridge and use within three months.

*Please ensure that any jam (jelly) jars you use for this recipe have been sterilized, otherwise the chutney will go bad. You can find out how to sterilize jars on page 118.

To decorate

Write a label and include the list of ingredients. Thread the label through a length of jute twine and tie it in a bow around the jar. Add a festive touch by sticking a piece of foraged greenery to the lid of the jar using washi/paper tape.

Blackberry & Bay Leaf Jam

I had always assumed jam (jelly) making would be a complicated process. The idea of sterilizing the jars and getting the right setting point seemed exhausting when it was a lot easier to buy a jar in the grocery store. I couldn't have been more wrong, as once you get the hang of it, it's very simple.

————————

You can use foraged blackberries for this recipe or use fresh or frozen berries from the supermarket. If you are using foraged blackberries, be mindful that some insects could be hiding in the leaves. Pop the berries into a strainer and give it a gentle shake. Remove any insects that may appear, then wash the berries thoroughly and leave to air dry.

Adding the bay leaves to the blackberries creates an almost floral, yet warming flavour. I used four small leaves picked from the bay tree in my garden, then dried. If you are using bay leaves from a packet, two will infuse the jam nicely.

I like to use glass jars with clip-top lids and rubber seals for preserving as these can be used repeatedly. You can also recycle old jam jars, but it's vital to use new lids and wax discs to ensure that no bacteria can enter the jar and spoil your jam. You can find new lids and wax discs in craft and kitchenware stores or online.

HOW TO STERILIZE

1. Preheat the oven to 130°C/250°F/gas mark

2. Wash jars, lids and seals in warm, soapy water, then rinse. Put the jars and the lids (if they are glass ones) on a baking sheet and put in the oven for 30 minutes. Sterilize rubber seals and metal lids by soaking them in boiling water.

3. The setting point for jam is 105°C (220°F). A jam thermometer is the easiest way to check that your jam has reached the correct temperature. Alternatively, you can use the wrinkle test (see How to step 4 on page 121).

4. As the jars need to sterilize for around 30 minutes, I pop my jars in the oven, then wait 15 minutes before I start heating my pan of fruit. After 15 minutes of boiling the jam, the jars will have had their 30 minutes and are ready to be filled.

Note
Don't add hot food to cold jars or cold food to hot jars as this can cause them to shatter.

continues overleaf...

Makes six small jars

Ingredients

1.5kg (3lb 5oz) blackberries

1kg (2lb 4oz) jam sugar

1 lemon, zested

4 tsp freshly squeezed lemon juice

Pinch of salt

2 dried bay leaves

HOW TO

1. Add the blackberries, jam sugar, lemon zest, lemon juice, salt and the bay leaves to a large, heavy-based saucepan or jam pan.

2. Bring to the boil, stirring until all the sugar has dissolved.

3. Lower the heat and simmer until the fruit is soft. This should take around 15 minutes.

4. If using a jam thermometer, turn off the heat at 105°C (220°F). If you are doing the wrinkle test, when you think the jam is ready, turn off the heat. Spoon a small amount onto a chilled saucer, allow it to cool (to avoid burning yourself) and then push your finger through the jam. If it wrinkles, it has reached the setting point. If not, turn the heat back on, simmer for five minutes and try again.

5. When the jam has reach temperature, remove the saucepan/jam pan from the heat.

6. Extract the bay leaves.

7. Optional: Press the jam through a sieve if you want to get rid of the seeds. Return to the saucepan/jam pan and reheat for around two minutes.

8. Decant the jam into the hot sterilized jars and seal.

9. Store in a cool, dark place. Once opened, keep in the fridge and use within three months.

To decorate

Write a label and include the list of ingredients. Thread the label through a length of jute twine and tie it in a bow around the jar. Add a festive touch by sticking a piece of foraged greenery to the lid of the jar using washi/paper tape.

Salted Caramel Fudge

This is one of my favourite recipes to make for gifts. It is unbelievably delicious, and to be honest, you'll probably have to stop yourself from devouring it! This recipe makes 36 squares, but you can easily double the quantities if you need to make more.

————

To package the fudge, I use old jam (jelly) jars* and add a pretty gift label along with a piece of velvet ribbon. You could also pop the pieces in one of the handmade gift boxes on page 75.

Makes 36 squares
Ingredients
200g (7oz) caster sugar
100g (3½oz) light muscovado sugar
2 tbsp glucose syrup
300ml (½ pint) double cream
125g (4½oz) unsalted butter
Sea salt flakes
½ tsp vanilla extract
1 tbsp icing (confectioner's) sugar

HOW TO

1. Grease and line a 20cm (8in) square cake tin (pan).

2. Place the caster sugar, light muscovado sugar, glucose syrup, double cream, butter, a pinch of sea salt flakes and the vanilla extract into a large saucepan.

3. Stir the mixture constantly over a low heat with a wooden spoon until the sugar has dissolved, and the butter has melted.

4. Turn up the heat slightly, then simmer for approximately 15 minutes, until the mixture reaches 113– 118°C (240°F) on the jam thermometer. If you don't have a jam thermometer, drop a little of the mixture into a bowl of cold water. The fudge will be ready once the mixture forms a ball in the water. If it's not at that point, continue simmering the mixture for a little longer and then test again.

5. Remove the saucepan from the heat and pour the mixture into a mixing bowl.

6. Leave to cool for 10 minutes.

7. Sift the icing sugar over the mixture, then beat with the wooden spoon for three to four minutes.

8. Spoon the mixture into the prepared cake tin and smooth the surface. Scatter a little more sea salt over the top.

9. Leave to cool, then pop in the fridge overnight.

10. Cut into squares and package.

11. Remember to include a gift tag with the list of ingredients.

*If you are using old jam (jelly) jars, be sure to clean them thoroughly in warm, soapy water before use. Add a piece of baking paper to gift boxes to help protect the fudge.

Chocolate Bark

If you have never eaten chocolate bark before, you are in for a treat. At its heart is a simple chocolate bar, but once you sprinkle on some extra treats, it is elevated to a thing of beauty. I find it difficult not to devour the whole bar once it's made, and often have to repeat the recipe to ensure I have enough left over for gifts!

――――――

I use a large bar of milk chocolate and swirl it through with the white to create a marble effect for this bark, but you can choose any number of combinations, or types of chocolate (dairy or non-dairy) for the base. My favourite toppings are dried fruits, nuts and caramel pieces as I love that crunchy chewiness you get when you eat all three together.

Use whichever toppings you prefer; I've included some further suggestions below. You can also add some spices to the chocolate as it melts: cardamom, cinnamon and chilli work well, or if you prefer a sweet and salty flavour, throw in a few flakes of sea salt.

Ingredients

400g (14oz) bar of milk chocolate
100g (3½oz) bar of white chocolate
75g (2½oz) chopped almonds
50g (1¾oz) sultanas
100g (3½oz) chopped caramel pieces

HOW TO

1. Line a baking tray/cookie sheet with baking paper and set aside.

2. Break up the milk chocolate bar into pieces and place in a heatproof bowl. Do the same with the white chocolate bar and place in another heatproof bowl.

3. Fill two saucepans roughly a third full of water and place on the hob (stovetop). Place the bowls of chocolate on top of the pans and turn on the heat.

4. Stir each bowl gently with a wooden spoon. Once the chocolate has melted, remove the bowls from the pans and turn off the hob.

5. Pour the milk chocolate onto the prepared baking tray/cookie sheet. Spread evenly.

6. Drizzle the white chocolate over the top of the milk chocolate. Using a bamboo skewer or a cake tester, swirl the white chocolate through the milk to create a marbled pattern.

7. Sprinkle over your chosen toppings and leave to set.

8. Break into shards.

Other topping ideas

* <u>Dried fruit</u>: Raisins, cranberries, cherries, candied peel, freeze dried raspberries, preserved ginger

* <u>Nuts</u>: Hazelnuts, walnuts, pistachios, pecans

* <u>Sweet additions</u>: Marshmallows, peppermint candy canes, popcorn, desiccated coconut, fudge pieces, cubes of marzipan

Finding Joy in Winter

KEEP FAIRY LIGHTS, CANDLES
OR A LANTERN IN A WINDOW TO
SHINE THROUGH THE BLEAK,
DARK NIGHTS OF WINTER.

Finding Joy in Winter

I used to loathe the time after Christmas. It was a period that brought financial stress and worry. Bills from overspending throughout December would arrive and the total on the credit card statement would be overwhelming. It would be constantly wet and cold, the windows dripping with condensation and wet washing would be strung over radiators.

Shops would send sales catalogues, and my emails would be pinging with offers for reduced items that I would find hard to resist. I tricked myself into believing that I needed new, shiny things for my home and wardrobe to make my life better, but it honestly just made everything harder as there was more clutter to deal with and my bank balance was left in ruins. It took me many years, but eventually I realised that buying lots of things didn't make me happy. I unsubscribed from retailers' emails, avoided going to stores and I only bought sale items if I needed to replace something.

I now embrace a kinder and gentler way of life during winter. There is nothing I can do to make the weather better, but every day, I wrap up warm and head out for a walk by the river and take in some fresh air. On dry, sunny days I bask in 'apricity' – enjoying the warmth of the winter sun on my face, and I pay close attention to the natural world, watching the plants and trees resting, preparing to unfurl their leaves once the soil starts to warm up.

Most days are spent working, but there are occasional trips to the cinema on cold afternoons. I cook nourishing bowls of lentil soup and serve them with homemade bread eaten in front of a roaring fire. New books from Christmas are read whilst tucked up under a warm blanket. Plans are made for the spring garden, and I linger over seed catalogues, choosing what I want to sow. I spend time learning a new craft or developing a skill. Tasks are usually completed whilst listening to podcasts on subjects I know little about.

I like to think of it as a season for quiet reflection and time to plan for the year ahead. Lean into the slower days, look after your physical and mental health, and prioritize rest before the busier, warmer months arrive once again.

———————

Wintering

Here in the UK most winter days are not sunny or snowy, but filled with grey skies and squally showers. The months after Christmas can feel endless, and many of us struggle with the lack of sunshine and constant drizzle. Winter can feel like a test of endurance. So, how can we make it more joyful?

———

* <u>Lean into hibernation</u>. Take your cue from nature, and allow yourself to rest, reflect and replenish your energy levels.

* <u>Prioritize sleep</u>. Get to bed early and enjoy the simple pleasure of a hot-water bottle. Turn off any screens at least an hour before bed.

* <u>Dress for the weather</u>. Wear warm, comfortable clothing. A good pair of thick socks, thermal underwear and a favourite jumper or cardigan make cold, wet winter days more bearable.

* <u>Digital detox</u>. Go on an information diet. Silence the online content or apps that affect your mood.

* <u>Do some gentle stretching</u> exercises every day. Pop on a YouTube video and engage in some mindful yoga or tai chi.

* <u>Get outdoors</u> as much as possible and enjoy 'apricity' – the warmth of the winter sun.

* <u>Eat warming foods</u> that contain ginger, turmeric, cinnamon and chillies. Cook hearty stews, soups and curries and add handfuls of leafy greens. Have a small handful of nuts, seeds and dried fruit for snacking, and include brazil nuts, which contain selenium, a mineral that helps support a strong immune system.

* <u>Keep to traditions</u>. Bake a 'galette de rois', a French cake made with puff pastry and filled with frangipane. Inside the cake hides a lucky charm *une fève*, and whoever finds the charm in their piece of the galette is named king or queen for the day. It is traditionally served on the 12th day of Christmas to welcome in the new year.

* <u>Find comfort in a soothing hot drink</u>. Try a spicy chai tea or indulge in a luxury homemade hot chocolate (see page 138 for the recipe).

* <u>Drink plenty of water</u>, if your home or workplace is centrally heated, to prevent your mucus membranes from drying up and making you more susceptible to viruses.

* <u>Take a daily vitamin and mineral supplement</u>, ideally one that contains 10 micrograms of vitamin D. This is an important vitamin as it helps keep our bones and teeth healthy. Throughout the summer our bodies take in vitamin D from sunlight, but the dark days of winter means we need to rely more on foods and supplements instead.

* <u>Leave a gentle light on</u>. Our homes always feel better when they are softly lit. Keep fairy lights, candles or a lantern in a window to shine through the bleak, dark nights of winter.

* <u>Enjoy quiet pleasures</u>, such as reading, journaling and star gazing.

* <u>Create a cosy corner</u> for reading, add a blanket to keep your legs warm and arrange candles in groups of three or five near where you are sitting.

* <u>Read a book</u> about the beauty of the winter season. Ask at the library or your local bookshop for recommendations.

* <u>Set yourself a reading challenge</u>. Work your way through a list of book prize winners or join a 'slow' reading group, where you take the time to ponder each sentence or chapter in detail and then discuss with other readers.

* <u>Gather with friends</u> or family for board game or movie nights. Set up your own book group and invite people to your home for food, wine and book talk.

* <u>Put together a collection</u> of family or friends' favourite recipes. Gather these into a binder or have it printed on eco-friendly paper and ink. Invite people round to cook and share their favourite meals from the collection. Photograph the memories and put together a keepsake album.

* <u>Take your time</u> making something or try a new craft. Learn how to draw or paint watercolours, or work with textiles and do knitting, weaving or quilting. Doing something creative is great for mental wellbeing.

* <u>Learn to mend</u>. Watch video tutorials to learn how to repair garments or try your hand at visible mending, where you make a feature out of the repair using patches or contrasting coloured thread.

* <u>Help others</u>. If you can already sew or knit, why not create items for charity? Hats, gloves, socks and blankets are always welcome at various charitable organizations.

* <u>Learn something new</u>. Sign up for a language course, research your family tree or do an online writing class.

* <u>Search for the signs of spring</u> around you. Look for buds on trees, snowdrops and crocuses emerging from the earth. Listen to birdsong in the woodland. Download an app that helps to identify different species.

* <u>Visit a nature reserve</u> or keep a nature diary. Invest in a lovely notebook to write down your finds.

* <u>Engage in a mindful photography walk</u>. Notice the small things in front of you, like the changing of the light, or the colours and textures of your surroundings. Take a photo when you feel ready, but don't worry about perfection.

* <u>Plant bulbs</u> in indoor pots. Muscari and paperwhite narcissus are beautiful in vintage terracotta pots, whereas hyacinths look wonderful in antique glass forcing vases. Search in charity shops or thrift stores for old casserole dishes or tureens and plant them up with primroses or winter pansies.

* <u>Treat yourself</u> to fresh flowers. A bunch of tulips, daffodils and hyacinths makes everything feel a little better on a dark, rainy day.

I WRAP UP WARM AND HEAD OUT FOR
A WALK BY THE RIVER AND TAKE IN
SOME FRESH AIR.

Wildlife Gifts

Birds and wildlife also appreciate a gift for winter. From my kitchen window, I love to watch the robins and blue tits darting nimbly from hidden spots deep within the surrounding hedge, then landing on the feeders that hang from the old boughs of the apple tree. It's easy to build wildlife a place to feast and shelter from things you may already have in the home. Here are a few ideas to get you started...

Pine cone bird feeder

Gather large pine cones from the woodland or forest floor (do not pick them from trees). If they are tightly closed, pop them in the oven for 10 minutes on the lowest temperature to open the branches. Attach a length of jute string or twine to the tip of the pine cones and spread unsalted peanut butter all over them. Pour some birdseed onto a plate and then roll the pine cones in the birdseed until they are completely covered. Hang outside from a tree or near a window so you can watch the birds feasting.

Orange-rind bird feeder

Cut an orange in half and scoop out the fruit, saving it to eat later. Using a pair of scissors, make a small hole near the top of the rind and the same on the opposite side. Cut a piece of jute string or twine and thread it through these two holes, tying the ends together to form a hanging loop. Fill the orange with birdseed and hang outdoors. To make landing and feeding easier, create a perch using skewers or small twigs. Push a skewer or twig into the rind to make a hole, then through the orange to make a hole on the other side. Repeat on the opposite side with the second skewer or twig to form a cross.

Bug hotel

Building a bug hotel in autumn (fall) provides beneficial insects and amphibians with a place to shelter, hide from predators or hibernate during winter.

The best bug hotels have lots of small spaces in different shapes and sizes. They should be made with materials that blend in with their natural surroundings and ideally be located in a shaded area near a tree or hedge.

Wall-basket bug hotel
This is a good way to utilize wall troughs and hanging baskets when summer displays have finished.

You will need
Wall trough or hanging basket

Pine cones

Dried leaves

Moss

HOW TO

1. Remove any liners from the trough or basket.

2. Fill the base of the trough or basket with a layer of pine cones.

3. Add a layer of dried leaves, then a layer of moss. Top with more pine cones until the trough or basket is filled.

Plastic-bottle bug hotel
Perfect for small spaces, including balcony gardens to attract ladybirds (ladybugs) and other mini-beasts.

You will need
Large plastic water bottle or milk carton

Scissors

Natural materials – pine cones, bamboo canes cut into small pieces, dried leaves, moss, small twigs

HOW TO

1. Carefully cut out a rectangular shape from one side of the bottle or carton.

2. Starting from the bottom, create layers from the natural materials.

3. Once it is filled from bottom to top, place in a warm and sheltered area.

Spiced Hot Chocolate

Enjoy a mug of this delicious hot chocolate in front of a roaring fire or to help warm you up while out on a wintery walk.

————————

Ingredients

450ml (15fl oz) milk (dairy or non-dairy)

45g (1½oz) light brown sugar

2½ tbsp good-quality cocoa powder (preferably fair trade and organic)

Pinch of salt

2 cinnamon sticks

2 star anise

½ tsp vanilla extract

¼ tsp ground ginger

HOW TO

1. Add the milk, light brown sugar, cocoa powder and salt to a small saucepan.

2. Turn on the heat gently and whisk all the ingredients until they are incorporated and there are no lumps.

3. Add the cinnamon sticks, star anise, vanilla extract and ground ginger to the pan. Bring the mixture to the boil, then reduce to a simmer.

4. Simmer for 10 minutes, whisking occasionally.

5. Remove the saucepan from the heat and allow to cool.

6. Leave the whole spices in for a stronger flavour, or remove once the mixture is cool.

7. Reheat to serve.

Resources

ONLINE SOURCES

* *The Spruce* Full of brilliant recipe ideas, decorating, gardening, crafts and green cleaning tips, The Spruce is a must read. thespruce.com

* *Ethical Consumer* An ethical consumer guide that provides detailed research and analysis of the products you purchase. They cover everything from make up and food to fashion as well as household cleaning products. ethicalconsumer.org

* *The Good Shopping Guide* Helping people to make informed decisions about which brands and companies are best for the planet, animals and communities. thegoodshoppingguide.com

* *Women's Voices for the Earth* A great resource that raises awareness of the damage toxic chemicals does to our homes, wellbeing and the environment. Includes handy factsheets about the toxins commonly found in cleaning products. womensvoices.org

* *Going Green* Lisa Bronner's website is packed with information on all aspects of natural living, but her tips for cleaning with castile soap are superb. As the mother of three children, she also shares practical advice for ethical and green family living. lisabronner.com

* *Friends of the Earth* Up-to-date news articles, features, political issues and campaigns in all areas of the environment and sustainable. living.friendsoftheearth.uk

APPS

* *Think Dirty* Comparison app for cosmetics and skincare which identifies what toxins are in products. thinkdirtyapp.com

* *Good on You* Ethical fashion app that checks how brands rate and compares them with others. goodonyou.com

PODCASTS

* *Low Tox Life* Looking at ways we can reduce toxins in all areas of our life. Alexx Stuart discusses diverse subjects such as GMO food, plastic pollution and saving the planet with experts in their relevant fields. lowtoxlife.com/podcast

* *The Tortoise* Brooke McAlary, author of Destination Simple, Slow and Care. My favourite writer and podcaster for all things slow and simple. brookemcalary.substack.com

* *As the Season Turns* by nature writer Lia Leendertz. Monthly episodes about seasonal changes and what to look out for. Covering everything from stargazing and wildlife spotting, to foraging recipes and folk tales.

* *Calm Christmas* by Beth Kempton. A weekly podcast that runs throughout the month of December and features recipes, how to decorate naturally and intentional gift giving advice. A lovely, cozy podcast to listen to in front of the fire.

DOCUMENTARIES

* *The True Cost Documentary* on fast fashion and the damage it can do to the environment. truecostmovie.com

* *A Plastic Ocean* Documentary on plastic waste in our oceans. plasticoceans.org

INSTAGRAM

* *@small_sustainable_steps:* For daily sustainable tips.

* *@carolyn_carter:* For simple and intentional living inspiration.

* *@junkaholique:* Artemis shares her beautiful home filled with budget friendly vintage and homemade treasures. Her Christmas posts are always inspirational, and I look forward to seeing how she decorates every year.

* *@blossomandbranchfarm:* A beautiful regenerative flower farm in Colorado. Briana makes gorgeous natural Christmas decorations, and her homemade dried flower advent calendar is particularly beautiful.

* *@simply.living.well:* Julia's account has long been a favourite of mine. Her simple style, home and garden is always inspiring, and her handy DIY's for making natural skincare products and eco-friendly candles are incredibly useful.

INSPIRING READING

* *Wintering* by Katherine May

* *Calm Christmas and a Happy New Year* by Beth Kempton

* *The Christmas Chronicles* by Nigel Slater

* *Nordic Winter Cookbook* by Viola Minerva Virtamo

* *Advent* by Anja Dunk

About the Author

Jen Chillingsworth is a freelance writer and photographer based in Dumfries and Galloway, Scotland. She worked in arts management before choosing to retrain as a market gardener. Here Jen discovered her love of plants, flowers, nature and the landscape, and how important it is that we try to protect them. She writes regularly about simple living, eating seasonally and making slow, sustainable changes to the home on her blog: jenchillingsworth.substack.com. Jen has written and photographed features published in *The Simple Things* magazine and *91 Magazine*. She has previously written four books for Quadrille, including the bestselling *Live Green*, published in 2019.

Acknowledgements

To Alan and Harry for your unwavering support, patience and understanding. You two are my favourite people in the world and I couldn't have written any of this without you.

To Mum, a huge thank you for all the knitwear! The beautiful jumper and mittens featured in this book were very kindly knitted by her and I'm lucky to be the recipient of many other gorgeous and warm winter sweaters.

To Mollie Dolly and Callum, thank you for the lovely drawings of Christmas that you both contributed to this book. Churros and ice cream are on me!

Thank you for the beautiful illustrations in this book which are by the very talented printmaker Sophie Elm. I'm delighted with how Sophie has captured a simple and slow Christmas. Please do check out her Instagram @_sophieelm_

And as always, thank you to the wonderful team at Quadrille publishing. I feel incredibly lucky to work with such talented and passionate professionals.

Managing Director Sarah Lavelle
Editorial Director Harriet Butt
Editorial Assistant Ellie Spence
Senior Designer Gemma Hayden
Photographer Jen Chillingsworth
Illustrator Sophie Elm
Head of Production Stephen Lang
Senior Production Controller Sabeena Atchia

Published in 2024 by Quadrille Publishing
Limited

Quadrille
52–54 Southwark Street
London SE1 1UN
quadrille.com

Cataloguing in Publication Data: a catalogue
record for this book is available from the
British Library

Text & photography © Jen Chillingworth 2024
Illustrations © Sophie Elm
Design and layout © Quadrille 2024

ISBN 978 1 83783 273 6

Printed in China using vegetable-based ink

FSC
www.fsc.org
MIX
Paper | Supporting
responsible forestry
FSC® C018179